A STUDY OF INDUSTRIAL WORKERS' CO-OPERATIVES

Copies of this paper may be obtained from The Economic and Social Research Institute (Limited Company No. 18269). Registered Office: 4 Burlington Road, Dublin 4

Price IR £5.00

(Special rate for students IR £2.50)

Robert O'Connor is Deputy Director of the Economic and Social Research Institute. Philip Kelly is an economist with Coras Trachtala (Irish Export Board). He was formerly a Research Assistant in the Economic and Social Research Institute. The paper has been accepted for publication by the Institute which is not responsible for either the content or the views expressed therein.

Printed by Cahill Printers Limited, East Wall, Dublin 3.

A STUDY OF INDUSTRIAL WORKERS' CO-OPERATIVES

ROBERT O'CONNOR

and

PHILIP KELLY

ISBN 0 7070 0027 0

CONTENTS

LIST OF TABLES

LIST OF FIGURES

Acknowledgements

The authors are greatly indebted to all the people and organisations listed in the appendix who supplied information relating to co-operatives in Ireland and in other countries. Special thanks are also due to the Industrial Development Authority (IDA) who sponsored this study and in particular to P. White, J. Kelly and P. Donnelly of that organisation who acted on a Steering Committee for the direction of the study and who contributed valuable suggestions and ideas. The other members of the Steering Committee were J. Dully of the Department of Industry, Commerce and Energy and J. Wallace of the Industrial Training Authority (AnCO). We wish to thank these also for their help, advice and constructive criticism.

Others to whom we are greatly obliged for having read earlier drafts and for making valuable suggestions are Seamus McKeon, Dublin, Denis Fitzpatrick of Kanturk, Co. Cork, Nora Herlihy, Dublin, founder of the Irish Credit Union Movement, J. McCarrick, Director General, ICOS, P. Mangan, formerly of ESRI, E. Honohan, Department of Economic Planning and Development, Paul Derrick, International Co-operative Alliance, Professors K.A. Kennedy, D.F. Hannan, Dr. D. Sapsford and K. Mellon, ESRI. We also wish to thank Brenda Forde for typing various drafts and Bernadette Payne and Mary McElhone for editing the script and seeing it through publication.

Any errors, omissions or misrepresentations are of course the sole responsibility of the authors.

General Summary

A workers' co-operative is the term used to describe an enterprise owned and controlled by those working in it. It is an advanced form of worker participation. Essential to the co-operative philosophy is the idea of equal partners working together for the common good. All co-operatives are built around a similar framework made up of six principles adopted by the International Co-operative Alliance in 1966. These principles can be summarised as follows.

1. Open, voluntary membership.
2. Democratic organisation on the basis of one member, one vote.
3. Limited interest on capital invested in the organisation.
4. Equitable distribution of earned surplus or savings, decided by the members, among co-operative development and education, common amenities to members, donations to charity, dividends to members or in other ways as the members may determine.
5. Education in co-operative principles and techiniques.
6. Co-operation among co-operatives.

While all co-operatives share the above basic values and principles, there are significant differences in the emphasis placed on each in different societies. This results in variations in constitutions, style and operational procedures. For example, members of co-operatives which were established as such from scratch will probably have a different philosophy and outlook from those who have converted an ailing capitalistic firm into a co-operative society. But regardless of the reasons for establishment, it is essential that a flexible view of what constitutes a co-operative be adopted. Indeed some enterprises are co-operative in name only, while others, although not called co-operatives are co-operative in spirit.

The idea of workers' co-operatives is not new, but in recent years there has been a renewal of interest in it. The main stimulus for this has come from what some people see as the apparent failure of existing systems, i.e., an unsatisfactory level of achievement on the economic objectives of full employment, price stability, living standards, and acceptable degrees of income and wealth distribution.

It is a reflection of the co-operative idea that people, both left and right of the political spectrum, see workers' co-operatives as a way of overcoming the problems of existing economic systems. It could be claimed that there is something in them for everyone. They can be held up either as proxies for an advanced form of socialism or as genuine examples of free enterprise.

Those who see co-operatives as solving most of the economic ills of society usually have in mind a complete labour managed system such as that in Yugoslavia. There are, however, few systems of this kind in the world and it would be difficult to create such in ordinary capitalistic societies. More usually therefore people see workers' co-operatives evolving as part of a mixed economic system and playing some part, though not perhaps a major one, in the creation of employment and income. It is in this context that they are considered here; we do not envisage a complete labour managed system in Ireland in the foreseeable future.

Advantages and Disadvantages of Workers' Co-operatives

Advantages

1. According to some writers the labour managed firm is better able than other kinds of business organisation to produce optimal incentive to work, and if everything else remained the same, this type of firm would be more pro-

ductive than any other.

2. Labour managed firms can be more efficient than capitalistic ones in avoiding market imperfections and lapses from competition. This arises because the co-operative can usually operate just as efficiently on a comparatively small as on a large scale. There is no need, therefore, why such firms would want to grow, since growth would not increase the income of its members. A capitalistic firm, on the other hand, would have every reason to grow because the bigger it becomes the greater its profits are likely to be. Consequently, once each labour managed firm has attained its optimum size there would be little or no tendency for it to grow bigger or to take over other firms. In an economy therefore with a large number of labour managed enterprises, other things being equal, there should be more firms and more competition.
3. Advocates of workers' co-operatives point to the fact that they are likely to provide the optimal incentives to work since people are working for themselves and thus stand to benefit directly from the firm's success. In these circumstances where there are no shareholders creaming off the profits there should be little labour management conflict and fewer strikes. This in turn should lead to greater productivity.
4. An important advantage of workers' co-operatives is that in times of recession they can help in maintaining existing levels of employment. In this situation, workers in a co-operative are more likely than those in a private or state owned firm, to undergo short-term sacrifices in order to keep the firm going.
5. The market system operating in free enterprise economies does not automatically generate full employment even in good times. Also it is growing more and more inefficient in recent years due to the frictions created by rapid technological change. The hazard therefore facing modern societies is that too many young people, in particular, may remain

unemployed far too long, thus creating a core of unemployable people, many of whom will develop anti-social habits. Different people have different ideas as to how this can be prevented, but there is now a growing body of opinion which holds that the surest way is to devise schemes which will encourage people through co-operative organisations to create jobs for themselves, either in industry or the services.

Disadvantages

Labour managed firms have a number of shortcomings. The more important are the following:

1. Many of them tend to be small and therefore suffer the problems of most small businesses.
2. A disadvantage which appears in most workers' co-operatives is under-capitalisation, reflecting the lack of finance which members can contribute and the lack of collateral which they can offer against borrowed funds. Students of co-operatives claim that the "Dilemma of Collateral" as it is called, is one of the most serious problems facing the system.
3. In the past many co-operatives have failed due to poor management and marketing expertise. This can happen for three reasons:
   (a) The workers in a co-operative are usually expert at producing goods but weak on organisation and marketing. If therefore the firm is too small to be able to afford specialised management, this function may have to be performed by an unqualified person.
   (b) The rules of many co-operatives specify that all members receive the same, or very nearly the same, income. Such firms cannot, therefore, pay high salaries for good management. If they do, it is by giving very high wages to all workers—skilled and unskilled alike.
   (c) Co-operatives tend to choose managers from among members and even if these know their jobs they may be unable to maintain the necessary level of discipline.

4. Many people with professional experience of business management are sceptical as to the possibility of combining democratic worker control and efficient management, and say that workers are likely to balk at redundancies or closures even if the health of the enterprise depends on them.
5. If the co-operative is a successful and expanding one, the committee may be loathe to take on new members as this would reduce the size of individual shares. Hired workers are therefore employed and eventually the co-operative may change into an ordinary company with the members as shareholders.

Workers' Co-operatives in Certain Countries

Great Britain

The modern formal British co-operative movement dates from 1844, when 28 poor weavers of Rochdale in Britain came together with capital of £1 each to open a small retail shop. They adopted a set of rules which were later to become enshrined as the Rochdale Principles and which today effectively guide the philosophy and conduct of co-operative societies all over the world.

In the early years of the movement, both producer and consumer co-operatives grew rapidly and by 1863 there were 454 societies in existence in Britain. A major blow came for the producer societies in 1870 when the movement was shaken by the failure of a number of societies, mainly in textiles, coal mining and engineering. Nevertheless, the thirty-year period from 1874 to 1905 was one of considerable expansion. The number of societies (excluding agricultural co-operatives) increased from 15 in 1874 to 109 in 1905, but from then onwards they declined to 48 in 1945 and to about 19 in 1977 with about 1,700 workers. The latter do not include the new co-operatives which were established with government support after a determined fight by workers to resist factory closure. Neither do they include what are known as the Industrial Common Ownership Movement (ICOM) firms, i.e., firms which have changed over from private enterprise to co-operatives in recent years and others which have started from scratch using ICOM model rules.

In 1978 there were 13 full member ICOM companies, a few of which are very large firms. Today there are over 300 such firms. The essential difference between ICOM firms and the older style producer co-operatives is that the former have a membership open only to the workers in the business. All firms adopt the principle of collective ownership which means that the assets are owned by the entire workforce as a group and as a group which changes with time. No individual has the right to draw on, or enjoy, a personal share of the assets and he receives no pay out (except a lump sum which is part of his pension rights) when he leaves. In the old style producer co-ops individual workers may hold shares in their societies, are entitled to interest on these and to withdraw their funds when they leave. Non-workers may also be shareholders.

The only survivor of three large worker take-overs promoted by the last British Labour Government is the Meriden Motor Bicycle Manufacturing Co. outside Coventry. The other two, The Scottish Daily News and Kirkby Manufacturing and Engineering have had to close down, though the latter operated for about five years. Meriden is also in a difficult position. A government grant of £4.2 million has to be repaid in 15 years and there are loans from other sources to be met as well. There are hopes, however, that it will survive.

Co-operation in Britain has been given an added impetus recently by a number of measures, most prominent of which is the Industrial Common Ownership Act 1976 which aims to provide financial assistance to productive enterprises which subscribe to co-operative principles. Up to £30,000 per annum for five years from 1976 can be given as a grant to any relevant body for the purpose of assisting that body to give advice about the organisation of common ownership and other co-operative enterprises. Grants and loans, up to £250,000 can also be given over five years from 1976 for the purpose of assisting a relevant body to make loans to co-operative enterprises. Examples of bodies who are availing of this assistance are the Industrial Common Ownership Movement, Industrial Common Ownership Finance Ltd., and the Scottish Co-operative Development Committee.

In 1978 the Co-operative Development Agency Act was passed. The Agency developed under the Act will attempt to fulfil its objectives by working with existing co-operative organisations. Government finance for co-operatives is also available under the Job Creation Programme (JCP) and many of the new co-operatives have been set up with JCP money. Another source of funds is the British Co-operative Bank. In 1978 the Chairman said that the bank was prepared, if necessary, to match pound for pound the joint investment of members of new worker co-operatives. A further monetary aid to co-operatives was contained in the 1976 Finance Act which gave exemption from capital gains and capital transfer tax to companies which are converting to a co-operative structure.

Spain—The Mondragon Movement

The Mondragon movement in Spain is in many ways the most interesting example of workers' co-operatives in capitalistic countries. Mondragon which is a small town in the Spanish Basque country, about 30 miles from Bilbao, has become the headquarters of a very large co-operative movement. Twenty-five years ago this district was a poor underdeveloped region. Today it is a thriving industrial centre. In the intervening period the co-operatives have grown into a group which employs roughly 16,000 people. There are agricultural co-operatives, a chain of co-operative stores, housing co-operatives and other educational institutions organised as co-operatives. There is a high-level co-operative research centre and an autonomous social welfare and insurance operation organised on co-operative lines. The great thrust of the group, however, is supplied by its industrial sector. At the end of 1978 there were 62 industrial co-ops employing more than 14,000 people. The group has at its centre a very successful workers co-operative bank: the Caja Laboral Popular (CLP). This bank mobilises the savings of people in the Basque province and uses as much of these as it prudently can for the creation and maintenance of employment in the co-ops. In banking terms alone it has been remarkably successful. As a mobiliser of savings it has out-performed almost all of Spain's regional banks but more important than the banking activities of the CLP is the work of its "Empressorial" or management division. This division is responsible for examining all new ventures and for a continuous monitoring of existing ones. It is doubtful if any comparable group of small and medium-sized enterprises has ever enjoyed such high level management back-up.

Other factors which help to explain the Mondragon success are:

1. A supportive community spirit, local patriotism, Basque Nationalism and a corresponding absence of bitter class divisions.

2. A positive legal and tax framework which the Mondragon Co-ops have taken advantage of.

3. A highly sophisticated set of democratically based structures covering, among other things, ownership by the workers, final control and fairly wide income differentials and

4. a network of mutually supporting co-ops rather than isolated individual ones. Among other things this has enabled the co-ops to offer an 80 per cent earnings guarantee to all their worker members and (so far at any rate) to avoid involuntary redundancies.

Israel

The strong co-operative movements in Israel are in the agricultural (including rural development) and consumer sectors. Despite nationalistic and other pressures, worker co-operatives have not flourished and attempts by the Histadrut (General Federation of Labour in Israel) to promote industrial democracy in its own plants, have, so far, been almost an entire failure. Workers' co-operatives have developed in more or less the same way as similar enterprises in other countries and suffered, more or less, the same vicissitudes of fortune. Financing, efficiency and managerial competency seem to generate the same problems everywhere.

In 1972 there were 87 workers' co-operatives in Israel with about 3,800 workers and an income of I £150.6 million.[1] Largest of these was the Haarqaz Co-operative which owns wood and metal working enterprises and accounts for 30 per cent of worker co-operative employees and income. It employs about 1,000 people, has an annual income of I £40 million, exports buses and various other products and produces packing crates for agricultural exports to the tune of about I £7.2 million. A high proportion of the employees are, however, hired workers. Other workers' co-operatives are 30 bakeries that supply 20 per cent of the country's standard bread. Unification of these small co-operatives seems necessary if they are to survive in face of vigorous competition from capitalistic giants.

Probably the most interesting workers' co-operatives in Israel are two large transport societies which between them account for 98 per cent of all public transport in Israel and are the oldest of their kind in the world. One of them undertakes all urban and the other all inter-urban transport. In 1972 the total numbers employed in these two co-operatives were 11,000 workers of which about half were members and the other half hired workers. At the beginning of 1977 the

[1]At the end of 1976, eight Israeli pounds were equal to one US dollar.

two decided to unite to become possibly the largest co-operative transport enterprise in the world. In addition to the transport industries, there are 19 haulage co-operatives employing 1,500 workers and carrying 50 per cent of all haulage in Israel.

Even though the public transport is carried on by co-operatives, this branch of the economy, in recent years, has had more or less the same problems as public transport in most countries. Because they are monopolies, the transport co-operatives are subject to strong governmental regulation with regard to fares and other matters. Such regulations have very complex side effects. One such effect seems to be that the financial position of the co-ops has deteriorated greatly in recent years. The immediate losses are met by loans and subsidies from the government but such funds do little to alleviate the causes of the trouble; if anything they partly account for them. It is claimed that the increased deficits are due mainly to wage rises granted to members in recent years. Had the wage increases for members been equal to those of the hired drivers, it is claimed that there would have been no deficit. The message from this is obvious. A co-operative when given monopolistic power acts in exactly the same way as an ordinary company, and when the government stands by to take up the tab, the co-operative has probably even fewer scruples than the company.

The most interesting modern development in Israel has been the industrialisation of the Kibbutzim (co-operative farms). Unfortunately these industries are based mainly on hired labour. At present about two-thirds of the Kibbutzim have industrial operations employing about 11,000 people. Many have several factories each, and in a few cases two or more Kibbutzim have combined to form large industrial units. There is a lesson in this for Irish Agricultural Co-operatives. They could go much further than at present in the organisation of rural development subsidiaries like building, drainage, water supply co-operatives etc., and thus do something about increasing employment in areas where they have been reducing it over the years through capital intensive rationalisation programmes.

Yugoslavia

After the Second World War the system of central planning was followed in Yugoslavia. As in all such economies the free market was abolished and prices regulated by the central authorities. Up to 1948 the country was strongly under the influence of the Soviet Union but friction, which had been developing for some time, came to a head with the Soviet economic and political blockade in that year. Stalin expected the blockade to break the resistance of Yugoslavia but Tito was able to mobilise the people to overcome these difficulties. For this, a generally accepted programme was needed and such a programme was the revival of the free market under a self-managed system which came into force by law in 1950.

Self management was first introduced in the production sector and some years later in the educational, health and similar institutions. A new constitution adopted in 1974 extended self management as an integral social system throughout the whole economy.

Because Yugoslavia is essentially a Communist state one must be wary of saying that its system of worker management could be adopted in a mixed economy. The real difficulty in such an economy would be in the abolition of private ownership, a step which would probably be resisted to the ultimate degree. The Yugoslavian example must therefore be taken with a good deal of reserve.

Nor has the system solved Yugoslavia's economic problems. According to government statements, the self-managed enterprises have been over-paying themselves in recent years and a total of 600,000 people had to face the prospect of a wage cut in November 1978. Strikes have occurred, and are occurring, in a number of large enterprises. The limit on the spread between maximum and minimum wages has led to the emigration of skilled workers and engineers. Inflation is also running very high.

These difficulties must, however, not be taken as an indictment of the co-operative system. Many people would argue that the Yugoslavian enterprises are not really co-operatives at all, since they lack one of the six basic principles of co-operatives, namely, open voluntary membership. In these circumstances the workers tend to view their firms more as state enterprises than as co-operatives.

France

The first French workers' co-operative was founded in Paris in 1834 by a group of gold jewellers but it was not until 1848 that other examples followed. Of the several hundred associations formed at this stage, few survived. Further associations were set up in the 1860s as a result of the availability of soft loans from the government of Napoleon III. Later in the 1880s still further associations were started. Again, few of these survived. The cause of failure lay in the very source of their establishment—the availability of easy access to finance meant that genuine worker's commitment from the bottom was absent.

Later initiatives came mainly from committed groups of artisans and some enterprises were set up following strikes or as rescue operations. Such initiatives have continued over the years so that the total number of French Co-operatives has been rising. In 1901 there were 119 firms; in 1978 there were 556. Of the latter, one-third were started prior to 1933. The French Co-ops are mostly small enterprises. Less than 20 per cent employ more than 70 people. Among the latter is one large enterprise manufacturing telephone equipment which employs 4,500 people, two building co-operatives employing 1,000 workers each, while a copper wire manufacturing unit has 675 workers. Total employment in French worker co-operatives is about 30,000 workers.

In 1975 almost half the French workers' co-operatives were

building and civil engineering enterprises while one-third were other engineering. Printing and newspapers accounted for about 7 per cent and services enterprises for another 7 per cent.

In France there is no formal requirement that all co-operative workers must be shareholders or that only workers can be members. As a result non-members accounted for as many as two-thirds of the labour force in 1975. However, the rights of the non-members are safeguarded by a requirement that not less than two-thirds of the Board of Administration must be workers. It is also laid down that in the event of liquidation, any surplus must not be shared out among members but must be passed on to other co-operatives. Furthermore there is a provision in French law which states that the workforce as a whole (whether members or not) must receive as large a share of profits as that allocated to shareholders in regard to their shares.

Italy

Italian co-operatives are affiliated to three different associations which represent three different political groupings. The Lega is a Communist group, the Confederation is a broadly Catholic Christian Democratic group while the Association reflects Republican/Social Democratic opinion. In the Lega group there are 1,425 co-operatives employing 110,000 workers. The Confederation group has 1,000 enterprises with about 32,500 workers while the association has 250 co-operatives with about 5,000 workers.

In most respects co-operatives of the three Italian groups can be treated as a single species. They operate under the same laws and share the same structures. Most workers are normally members. The members in general meeting elect a policy-making board. The board in turn appoints the management. Capital subscriptions vary from a nominal £5 to the equivalent of three months starting salary in some cases. Under Italian law, members may only receive interest on their subscriptions. No bonus share-outs are allowed.

Among the Italian co-operatives are a number of large building firms. Other smaller societies produce optical and dental equipment, weighing machines, lifts, mining equipment, machine tools, grain driers and fruit grading equipment. There are co-operatives also in the textile, clothing and shoemaking trades. Transport co-operatives are in existence in Italy as well as in France while there are service co-operatives of various kinds such as fire watching, diving and security services.

The Italian co-operatives appear to be the best developed in the western world but there is some doubt about the validity of the statistics. Also there is a certain amount of scepticism as to whether many of the large groups are real co-operatives at all.

Denmark

Denmark is unique in respect to the relationship between the trade unions and the co-operative movement. One of the objectives of the trade union movement since 1907, has been to provide a form of co-operative organisation as an alternative to private enterprise. Through this, workers can achieve various economic objectives such as job security, management control, protection of consumer interest and support in the struggle against multinational corporations. Towards this end the Central Union of Urban Co-operative Societies (DkF) was founded in 1922. Both the Trade Union Federation and the Social Democratic Party have seats on the DkF.

Currently there are 653 societies affiliated to the DkF. Of these, 490 are housing societies, 65 are building co-operatives, 49 are canteens; there are 18 bakeries, 5 oil and fuel co-operatives and 30 miscellaneous societies. The housing societies employ 3,500 full-time and 2,500 part-time staff. About 5,000 workers are employed in the building co-operatives. The National Association of Canteens employ some 250 workers and serve meals to about 20,000 employees of other companies. The co-operative bakeries supply 27 per cent of the bread market and employ 800 workers. Among the miscellaneous societies is a Workers' Co-operative Bank which is the sixth largest bank in Denmark. The miscellaneous and fuel-oil co-operatives employ about 1,800 workers so that total employment in all workers' co-operatives in Denmark is about 14,000 people.

There is no co-operative legislation in Denmark; co-operative societies of all kinds are registered under ordinary company law. The DkF, however, (as well as all other co-operative federations) has its own rules which state that every disagreement in a workers' co-operative shall be resolved by negotiations and not by strikes or lock outs. DkF also encourages workers to hold shares in their co-operatives but there is limited interest on such shares and they are redeemable only in the event of death or liquidation. No allowance is made for inflation on redeemed shares.

Trade unions have contributed to the financing of all workers' co-operatives in Denmark usually through the workers' co-operative bank. Another source of finance is the Co-operative Finance Fund (AKF) which was started in 1953 by the Labour Movement (LO), DkF and the Workers' Co-operative Bank. In 1977 AKF had assets of 19.9 million kroner of which some 16.6 million kroner were invested in 40 workers' co-operatives.

Co-operatives in Ireland

Northern Ireland

There are a number of community co-operatives in Northern Ireland but there are very few enterprises in the area which could be described as workers' co-operatives. An interesting development, however, has been the appointment by the Local Enterprise Development Unit (LEDU) of an Industrial Co-operative Adviser whose function is to educate, advise and financially assist groups of people wishing to establish industrial workers' co-operatives or to change over from private enterprise to co-operatives. It is understood that some developments in this regard are in course of being finalised.

Republic of Ireland

At present there are only four real industrial workers' co-operatives in the state, most of which are quite small in size. These are The Graphic Arts Society in Dublin which is engaged in process engraving, Crannac Co-operative in Navan, which manufactures high class furniture, Irish Springs and Castle Shoes in Dundalk which manufacture bed springs and shoes respectively. Total turn-over in these enterprises in 1977 was about £2 million and total employment was 130 people. All of these co-operatives except Graphic Arts were formed from companies which had closed down and were taken over by the workers. Another company, Bewleys in Dublin, has been established as a member of ICOM and handed over by the owners to the workers. It is now carrying on as a successful co-operative.

The workers in the Clover Meats Agricultural Co-operatives in Waterford, Clonmel and Wexford have subscribed £120,000 in share capital to the co-operative and have been given representation on the Board of Management. It is envisaged that other agricultural co-operatives will adopt similar structures so as to ensure harmonious relations between the farmers who supply raw materials and the plant workers who process them.

In addition to the above there are a number of other development co-operatives in the West of Ireland, the best known being Glencolumbkille in Donegal, Tormasheady, Co. Mayo, Cois Fharraige, Connemara, The West Kerry Development Co-op, Dingle and Slieve Bawn in Strokestown, Co. Roscommon. These operate tourist development centres, craftworks, Irish colleges, vegetable and fish processing, lamb fattening, deep ploughing and printing works. None are, however, closed worker co-ops.

Conclusions

Part of the pressure for workers' co-operatives comes from the supposition that they are able to protect or create employment. In a liberal western style situation where unions tend to keep wages at a relatively high level and employers counter this by displacing workers through mechanisation, there is need for some system which concentrates on employment creation. The co-operative seems to have a comparative advantage in this regard. It can, if required, adjust its wage levels to competitive levels and in addition it probably can avoid strikes and other industrial actions to a greater extent than other firms.

In practice very few days are lost in co-operatives due to strikes, and on the basis of this behaviour it is often argued that co-operative organisation of industry would ensure industrial peace. All students of industrial relations would not accept this view. There is now definite evidence that strike proneness is a function of size of business. If there are a large number of people in a single plant and if its operation depends on all of them being at work, then this fact must inevitably lead to an unacceptable high level of strikes. "The bigger the crowd the greater the chance of a fight". Despite this analysis we are of the opinion that for any given sized firm the co-operative has a better chance of having industrial peace than private or state enterprises.

The organisation of economies on co-operatives lines has sometimes been suggested as a means of controlling inflation. There is no evidence, however, to support this view which is based on the premise that inflation is caused mainly by wage increases. As is now well known there are many other factors involved and, indeed many of these are outside the control of individual firms and even of governments. It is in maintaining employment in times of depression and high inflation that co-operatives have an advantage rather than by preventing inflation.

The situation regarding the efficiency of co-ops *vis-à-vis* other forms of business organisation is unclear. Sometimes co-operatives appear to be more efficient than capitalistic firms and there is some evidence to suggest that success is positively associated with degree of participation. In co-ops where the workers take an active interest in running the business, efficiency appears generally to be high and vice versa. However, just like other businesses the performance of co-ops is uneven and much additional work must be done before definite conclusions regarding efficiency can be reached.

With regard to motivation, our researches tend to show that co-operatives are children of distress and tend to arise because the usual capitalist system is not providing a solution, or when a trade or industry is in decline. Often co-operatives are formed to fulfil some religious, political or philosophical ideal and still others are formed, in regions suffering deprivation, as the only means of generating enthusiasm and motivation among people. The important point to note in this connection is that the co-operatives so formed have tended to maintain employment in the areas and firms where established, and have tended to relieve a great deal of human misery. Even in the recent depression, the large British government co-operatives, Meriden and KME (though the latter has now folded up) served a very useful purpose. They maintained employment for over 1,000 people who would otherwise have been out of work. And though the cost to the state has been high, it has probably been much less than would have been paid out in unemployment benefits and social welfare allowances. These and many other similar societies have therefore done well in continuing to operate until economic conditions generally have improved.

Potential for Co-operative Enterprise in Ireland

If previous experience of workers' co-operatives in the UK and Ireland were extrapolated, we might expect societies to remain restricted to a relatively small number of industries where the economics of large scale production had not yet penetrated and capital investment was less important than skilled labour in producing the final product. In this situation the prospect of establishing viable co-operatives would be a very gloomy one. There are, however, some more encouraging features which should be mentioned.

It is believed that in future years basic industry will be less important than at present as an income and employment generator while the service sector will grow. In this situation there would be a wider scope than at present for the development of workers co-operatives since service units are more easily organised and usually require less capital than manufacturing firms. There is scope therefore for co-operatives in many areas in Ireland such as in the business of subcontracting for construction firms, interior decorating, sign painting, business management consultancy etc. There is scope also for the development of industrial co-ops in the food industry on the lines of that in Clover Meats. Another suitable area for co-operative development is in the underdeveloped rural districts where the whole community needs to be organised if economic development is to be achieved. There is also scope for co-operatives in inner city areas where there are large pools of unemployed young people.

Best Co-operative Structure

Co-operatives may be formed under a number of different legal structures but it is our opinion that new workers' co-operatives should be established under the Industrial and Provident Societies Acts (IPSA) unless there is some specific reason for selecting an alternative structure. Many experienced co-operators are of opinion that the main thing is to have flexible legislation since the aims of members vary considerably depending on circumstances; the IPSA provides such flexibility. The rules adopted by a society should, however, be very specific and particularly in regard to investment by members in the co-op. Generally speaking, all workers should have to contribute some minimum sum either through payment, or by deduction from wages and they should receive a reasonable rate of interest on these investments. Surpluses, after allowing for interest on shares and reserves, should be distributed to the workers and not to other shareholders, i.e., retired workers or outsiders.

Additional Services for Co-operatives

If workers co-operatives are to come into operation in Ireland, good organisation and much help and guidance is required. To ensure that these conditions are at least partially fulfilled, some kind of a workers' co-operative agency is required. This might be established and operated by the National Co-operative Council (NCC) but regardless of whom the organisers are, some government aid will be required for the acquisition of premises and the payment of staff. Formal structures will also need to be established so that financial and other provisions can be co-ordinated with various state and semi-state bodies like the Department of Labour, IDA, AnCO, County Development teams etc. The agency, when started, should appoint a Development Officer whose duty it would be to organise and appraise industrial projects and advise on how applications for grants and other state aids should be made. He should also advise on the conversion of private firms to co-operatives. It is envisaged that grants for industrial projects should come from the IDA, Gaeltarra Eireann, Shannon Free Airport Development Company Limited (SFADCO) and ICC. We understand that the IDA is prepared to offer the same level of funding to viable workers' co-operatives as it is to private firms. We do not envisage any modifications of IDA services which need to be made to take account of the unique features of workers' co-operatives. The existing services can cope adequately with these enterprises except, of course, for service co-operatives. For various reasons the IDA cannot normally fund such enterprises, hence, money for these will have to come from other sources such as the banks, credit unions or from the Central Development Committee's Special Regional fund.

Chapter 1

Introduction

In the Green Paper "Economic and Social Development 1976-1980" (1976) and subsequent government documents on the economy, a change over to co-operative enterprise has been mentioned as one of the measures which could help in promoting productivity. The objective is to associate employees more closely with the enterprise and its financial results. It is thought that this type of organisation could assist firms facing adaptation problems and financial difficulties as well as helping to sponsor new projects on co-operative lines.

Though the idea of workers' co-operatives is not new it seems to be gaining momentum throughout the world in recent years. In addition to Yugoslavia, where the whole economy is based on the co-operative idea, there are strong movements in many countries including centrally planned economies. However, the extent to which all of these are true worker co-operatives is open to some doubt. The movement in the Republic of Ireland is still very small.

The interest of the authors of this paper in workers' co-operatives stems from the belief that such organisations could help in solving some of the intractable difficulties which seem to be inherent in our economic system such as:

1. the mounting level of unemployment throughout the developed world and the difficulty of creating work opportunities, especially for young people whose expectations have been raised by extended academic education.

2. the problem of industrial unrest and the associated troubles of strikes, lock-outs, etc., and
3. the problem of inflationary pressures which seems to be endemic in modern society.

With regard to unemployment, there seems to be a body of opinion which holds that the surest way to overcome this difficulty is to devise schemes which will encourage and help people to create jobs for themselves either in industry or in services. It is often suggested that this can be done through the co-operative movement. The experiences in this regard with co-operatives, both in Ireland and abroad, are investigated in the paper.

On the question of industrial unrest, many people are now saying that real work motivation can only be engendered by giving workers greater participation in the management of their enterprises. This would ensure, on the one hand, that the enterprise was managed in the workers' interests, and, on the other, that they stood to benefit directly from its success. Campbell *et al.* (1977) say that the main argument is now over how this participation should be achieved, whether through profit-sharing schemes, worker representation at board level or through an extension of the worker co-operative sector.

Discussing inflationary pressures Jay (1976) has argued that it will be necessary to organise industry on a co-operative instead of a capitalistic basis if inflation is to be brought under control. He says that our political economy is inherently unstable, because it insists upon a level of employment which is unattainable without accelerating inflation under existing labour market arrangements. Therefore these arrangements must change in such a way as to enhance the general efficiency of the labour market. The only potentially acceptable alternative, as Jay sees it, is a change in company law which gives ownership and ultimate control of enterprises to the people employed by them. They would then have to sink or swim in a market environment. In these circumstances inflation would subside; and employment would be high. On an *a priori* basis, Jay's suggestions seem convincing but whether they would be effective in practice is another matter.

Jay is not alone in his views on this matter. The Majority Report of the Working Group on a Co-operative Development Agency in Britain (HMSO, 1977) suggested that co-operatives could "contribute to a solution of many current problems" and might "bring advantages of special value to the resolution of the country's economic problems".

These and many other issues are of crucial importance in modern economies and we refer to them in more detail in the final chapter after examining the workers' co-operative movement in a number of countries.

Outline of this Study

In carrying out the study we have:

A. Discussed the principles and practices of the co-operative system and outlined its theoretical advantages and disadvantages as compared with other systems.
B. Reviewed the historical development of workers' co-operatives in a number of countries, including Ireland.

As a result of this review we attempt, in the concluding chapter, to answer the following questions.

1. The extent to which a widespread development of workers' co-operatives might help in solving the problems of unemployment, industrial unrest and inflation.
2. How efficient are co-operatives in comparison with other forms of industrial organisation?
3. How far non-economic motivations have played a part in the establishment of successful co-operative movements and whether the continuance of such motivation is necessary to the success of the movements.

In addition to answering these questions we have

attempted to determine:

4. (a) the potential in Ireland for new enterprises (both industrial and service) based on the co-operative structure.
   (b) if there are some industries and services having certain characteristics which are likely to be more suitable for co-operative organisation than others.
   (c) if there are particular combinations of workers available offering good prospects for success in this area.
   (d) if there are any modifications of IDA services for new firms which need to be made to take account of the unique features of worker co-operatives.
   (e) what services would be required by workers who wished to form co-operatives or to turn existing businesses into co-operatives?
5. What is the best corporate or internal organisation structure for co-operatives, i.e., the usual co-operative structure, ordinary company structure, or a new co-operative structure? There are many who would argue that the co-operative idea is too restrictive, that ordinary company rules would give more freedom of operation.
6. The study also investigates the prospects for employment in rural areas through the formation of rural development co-operatives and whether the present agricultural co-operatives could be more broadly based to include the workers as well as the suppliers of raw materials (the farmers).

Procedure of the Study

In order to investigate the various issues cited above, the authors visited various co-operatives and people interested in the idea in Ireland and other countries to examine at first hand what was happening. Co-operative managers in the Republic and Northern Ireland were asked to complete a questionnaire eliciting information on how their enterprises came into operation, how they were financed, the size and structure of the workforce, nature of products produced, profitability of operations, methods of organisation, wages and salary structure, industrial relations problems, etc. A copy of the questionnaire is available in the ESRI for those who are interested.

It should be stated that no attempt is made in the report to give a comprehensive account of the industrial co-operative movement throughout the world. To do so would involve much more time and resources than were available. The purpose was to obtain a picture of what was happening in fairly typical countries and to sketch the problems which had been encountered in these areas. To do this we chose the following countries where workers' co-operatives are fairly well developed, Yugoslavia, France, Italy, Denmark, Spain, Israel and Britain in addition to Northern Ireland and the Republic of Ireland where the movement is in its infancy. Omitted is Malta which in recent years appears to have organised a strong self-managed sector but about which we knew little until the publication of a book on the subject, at the time this publication was going to press (Kester, 1979). This book states that by mid-1979 almost one-third of the wage and salary earners in Malta had formally instituted forms of participation.

In describing the workers' co-operative movement in the different countries we have, where it was thought necessary, given some detail regarding other forms of co-operatives so as to put the workers' movement in context.

Chapter 2

The Structure and Operation of Workers' Co-operatives

An industrial co-operative can be regarded as an advanced form of worker participation. Under the orthodox form of worker participation a few workers are chosen to act on the Board of Directors. In a workers' co-operative the enterprise is owned and controlled entirely by the workers.[2] Because the business is controlled by the workers these societies are often referred to as *closed co-operatives* in contrast to agricultural and other societies where membership is open to non-workers, and workers are seldom members.

According to the International Co-operative Alliance (ICA) (1966) all co-operatives are formed around a framework of six basic principles which can be summarised as follows:

1. Open voluntary membership.
2. Democratic organisation on the basis of one member, one vote.
3. Limited interest on capital invested in the organisation.
4. Equitable distribution of earned surplus or savings as between co-operative development and education, common amenities to members, donations to charity, dividends to members or in other ways as the members may determine.
5. Education in co-operative principles and techniques, and
6. co-operation among co-operatives.

In a classical book on the subject of co-operatives, Jaroslav

[2]In practice, of course, there are often some outside members as well.

Vanek (1970) of Cornell University[3] elaborates at length on these principles with which he appears to be in substantial agreement. He says that the co-operative or labour managed firm has five main characteristics as follows:

The first and most important is that the enterprises are controlled and managed by those working in them. Participation in control and management extends to all the workers and is on the basis of equality, each worker having one vote, irrespective of his position in the firm. The right to control and manage derives from work rather than from ownership and in this regard the labour-managed firm differs from the agricultural co-operatives, where the ultimate source of authority springs from ownership rather than from participation in the work of the firm. A very significant and practical implication follows from this, namely, the traditional labour contract whereby a man sells or rents out a certain number of hours of his work per day is entirely abolished. A proper co-operative should not hire a man on such a basis in the traditional sense of the word. The significance of this principle cannot be overemphasised; one of the strongest forces which have undermined efforts in the past to create self-managed firms has been the hiring of "second class workers" (i.e., workers who are not members) under a wage contract. Almost without exception the eventual result of this practice has been the degeneration of the participatory firm into an ordinary joint stock company.

The second characteristic of the labour-managed firm is that the workers share in the income of the enterprise on an equitable basis. This means that the shares must be agreed by all and that equal shares go to labour of equal intensity and quality. Thus while income distribution within the firm would probably be more egalitarian than it is under a capitalistic system it would not be egalitarian in any absolute sense.

[3]Vanek, who is Professor of International Studies at Cornell University, is one of the leading authorities in the world on the theory and practice of workers' co-operatives.

Vanek's third characteristic is that the members of the working community do not own the capital assets used by the firm. Ownership resides in the firm considered as a legal entity. The working community enjoys the fruits of the production of plant, equipment, buildings, etc., but pays a fee or rental of some kind for their use. It follows from this that the working community cannot sell or destroy the real assets of the firm but, at the same time, the lenders of capital have no control over the use of the assets of an enterprise either. So long as the community meets whatever debt servicing obligations it contracts for, it retains control over all the assets. The members of the firm should be motivated in the firm as a place of work and source of livelihood and not in any possible capital interests such as capital gains or opportunity to accumulate personal wealth. Ideally, all funding should come from outside the firm; the debt should be perpetual and no individual should have any equity ownership in the firm.[4] The members must never be allowed to own or dispose of any of the assets of the business. The history of co-operatives is replete with examples of the unfortunate consequences of equity ownership. Many plywood co-operatives in the USA (which started as genuine co-operatives) are in the process of being converted into capitalistic firms because the original worker owners were allowed to acquire shares in the firm and employ secondary workers (Bellas, 1972). The average share is now worth $30,000-$50,000 and there are obviously few young workers able to buy shares of such value. This characteristic seems to derive from Vanek's own views on co-operative organisations, it is not inherent in the ICA's six basic principles and many writers, including the authors of this paper, are strongly of the opinion that workers should have a stake in their businesses. The dangers

[4] By this Vanek means that the workers do not invest directly in the firm. Ideally their shares should be invested in a co-operative bank from which the co-operative firm borrows. This prevents retired workers from bankrupting the firm by heavy withdrawals.

of not having a stake are greater than of having one, and of eventually owning the firm.

The fourth characteristic is that the labour-managed firms envisaged by Vanek operate in a market economy. What this means is, that transactions between various decision-making units are settled through the ordinary process of buying and selling, lending, borrowing, renting, hiring, etc. All units act freely and prices serve the function of equating supply with demand. The national economy may be composed entirely of such units as is the case in Yugoslavia, or there may only be a small number, but in either case the pattern of production and distribution is settled through a great number of individual low level decisions rather than through a small number of high level ones as would be the case in a centrally planned society.

The fifth characteristic is the principle of freedom. It has two aspects. On the one hand, the individual is free to take, not to take, or to leave a particular job. On the other hand, the firm is free to hire or not to hire a particular individual. If it wishes, however, the working community can limit its powers to dismiss a person even where strict economic considerations might call for doing so.

Reviewing Vanek's works, Professor David O'Mahony (1973) of University College Cork says that the workers' co-operative is a legal entity existing by virtue of its being created in law. It (the firm) owns the real assets, the fruits of which the working community enjoys, but nobody owns it (the firm). In this respect it differs from a joint stock company, agricultural producers' co-operative or nationalised industry, but is very similar to an institution such as the university or to certain irrevocable trusts. In an agricultural producers' co-operative the members own the assets and can dispose of the shares anytime they wish. The university community, on the other hand, has the right to control, manage and use classrooms, laboratories, etc. but does not own them.

The university has the right to hire or lease capital assets but has no right to control their use.

Support Structure

For a self-managed system to be established a number of supporting efforts would be needed. According to Bayard *et al* (1974), an associate of Vanek at Cornell University, if the co-operative is to survive it must have the capacity to accumulate and/or attract investment funds. In order to facilitate this process there should ideally be a separation of the functions of accumulation and funding, on the one hand, from the function of production, and work on the other. In the early stages of self-management the latter function should generate investment resources, but these should not remain under the direct control of the self-managed community, they should be transferred to a supporting corporation, which serves as a funding institution for a large number of self-managed firms. Such a body can collect savings from individual members, including pension funds, but in the initial stages, at any rate, it would need to have some government support because it will have little in the way of collateral to offer its lenders.

The basic functions of the supporting corporation are to accumulate a capital base for the self-managed community, to acquire investment capital from the external capital market, to use this capital to provide financing for self-managed corporations and to ensure that self-managed firms operate according to the basic principles of self-management. Thus it operates essentially as a financial intermediary which, owing to its capital base and the diversification of its investment, can more readily attract external capital than individual self-managed firms and act as an instrument of broad community control over a number of federated self-managed corporations without interference in actual production decisions.

A successful effort to develop self-managed firms in any country must also include an education effort, both for those belonging to the self-managing sector and for those outside it. After some ten generations, capitalism in the western world has succeeded in indoctrinating most people with the capitalistic spirit. For self-managed firms to emerge, the impact of this process must be lightened or at least put in context. The best way of doing this is through education. This educational effort could be launched at two levels. First, introductory lessons on co-operation should be given in the primary school curriculum. Secondly, a national institute for study and education in self-management could, through its research, contribute to the development of the most optimal industrial organisation. The educational aspects cannot be over-stressed. After years of working with, and advising co-operatives, Vanek says that the educational effort is the most important requirement for success. It is a necessary condition. Without it a viable co-operative movement cannot come into existence.*

Practical Problems of Financing Co-operatives

The views of Vanek and Bayard on the financing of co-operatives are somewhat idealistic as they presuppose the presence of a supporting financial corporation. In most countries such an institution is not in existence and in these circumstances new co-operatives must raise as much share capital as they can, directly from their members (Derrick, 1978). Unfortunately co-operative production societies have usually been formed by people with very limited resources and they have sometimes had to raise a good deal of the share capital needed from outside sources. Such outside shareholding can mean that a co-operative is not wholly controlled by worker members and this can affect members' involvement and sense of common purpose. It also means that the co-operative is paying very high financial charges which makes it very vulnerable in recession conditions.

Derrick says that all enterprises need a certain amount of

*Personal communications, August 1977.

"own capital" before they can borrow, and rules which prevent investment by workers in their business are flying in the face of co-operative experience. The model rules of the Common Ownership Movement in Britain (of which Bewley's in Dublin is a member) restricts shareholdings to a £1 share per member so that practically all capital has to be borrowed. This creates few problems for those co-operatives which are converted from successful private businesses with a good capital structure; but for others there are many obvious difficulties in raising capital.

Effect of Co-operatives on the National Economy

In the previous sections we have been concerned primarily with the organisation and operation of the labour-managed firm. We turn now to the implications of self-management for the economy as a whole. Vanek (op. cit.) claims that there is an inherent tendency in the participatory economy[5] towards the avoidance of the kind of general unemployment that characterises an economic depression in a capitalistic economy. The reason for this is that the residual income goes to labour rather than to profit. Though money income may fluctuate widely from time to time, employment and output are likely to remain comparatively stable over the long run.

The truth of this may be seen by looking at what happens in agriculture, a sector where the residual income goes primarily to labour. The vast majority of farmers being self-employed are in much the same position as the participants in the labour managed enterprise. If, for any reason, such as a fall in the price of farm products, farmers' receipts fall temporarily, there are no repercussions on employment. All that happens is that the farmers' own residual income falls too. In the case of an enterprise with a hired labour force, on the other hand, a fall in receipts, whatever the cause, will

[5] A participatory economy is one like Yugoslavia where all the firms are self-managed.

normally lead to a reduction in the labour force and a consequent cutback in output in an attempt to maintain profit or minimise loss. This in turn gives rise to secondary effects and soon leads to general unemployment and depression.

In a participatory economy price fluctuations should be primarily short-run phenomena. A small self-managed sector in an otherwise conventionally organised economy could not, of course, isolate itself from the inflationary pressures that seem to be almost inescapable in capitalistic economies. But if the whole economy were organised on a participatory basis the absence of upper pressure on wages and salaries, on the one hand, and the pervasiveness of competition, on the other, should go far towards eliminating inflationary pressures in the long-run. This question is discussed in the final chapter.

Vanek (1971) argues, however, that the spontaneous emergence of a full-scale labour-managed economy is unlikely for several reasons. The most important of these is what he calls "the dilemma of collateral". This is the reluctance of the various lending institutions to lend without security. Another obstacle is that those with vested interests in the present economic system would in all probability oppose the co-operative idea in a variety of ways. If a labour-managed economy or sector of an economy is to come into being, Vanek says that it must be encouraged by the government[6] and at least four requirements must be fulfilled in order to make it viable. These are:

1. The labour-managed section would have to reach a certain minimum size or "critical mass" since the survival of isolated labour managed firms is improbable. Even if a few firms did survive, the beneficial effect they would have on the economy would be negligible.
2. Firms in the labour-managed sector would have to

[6]It should be stated that the Mondragon movement in Spain was started initially without government support.

receive equality of treatment compared with other firms in the sense that they should not be discriminated against.

3. The labour-managed firms would have to be given a clear and well-defined legal status for the purpose of taxation, making contracts, liability in the event of failure and so on.
4. An institution to serve the needs of the labour-managed section would have to be established, whose main functions would be:
   (a) to serve as the principal source of external finance, thereby preventing the "dilemma of collateral" from arising.
   (b) to secure equal treatment for the labour-managed firms, and
   (c) to pursue a lending and investment policy designed to ensure that the "critical mass" would be reached.

Despite what Vanek says about the necessity for a minimum "critical mass", Barkai (1978) states that there may be a place for a small number of co-operatives in many countries to cater for the people who are not motivated by material incentives to the same extent as the majority of people.

Theoretical Advantages and Disadvantages of the Labour-Managed System

Advantages

According to the theorists the labour-managed firm is better able than other kind of business organisations to produce optimal incentives to work. There is a stronger tendency for labour effort to be greater in labour managed than in other types of economic systems and if everything else remained the same, including managerial and entrepreneurial capacities, the labour-managed economy would be more productive than any other. This increased productivity can, however, have a two-edged effect and may result eventually in a change in the status of the co-operative. With high income *per capita*, as a result of high productivity, members of the co-operative may be loathe to admit new members in case their average revenue would fall. "Second class" workers may be employed while the original members keep control of the assets and become a board of directors.

Labour-managed firms can be more efficient than capitalistic ones in avoiding market imperfections and lapses from competition. This arises because the co-operative can usually operate just as efficiently on a comparatively small as on a large scale. There is no need therefore why such firms would want to grow, since growth need not increase the income of its members. A capitalistic firm, on the other hand, has more built-in stimuli for growth. Consequently, once a labour-managed firm has attained its optimum size there would be less tendency to grow bigger or to take over other firms. In the participatory economy, therefore, other things being equal, there should be more firms and more competition. According to O'Mahony, (op. cit., p. 42) maximisation of profits per firm promotes the growth of firms to the maximum size consistent with efficiency, while maximisation of income per worker (the goal of a co-operative) keeps firms at the minimum size consistent with efficiency.

Disadvantages

The labour-managed system has a number of theoretical shortcomings. Of these, the possible absence of an incentive to expand production in the short-run in response to an increase in demand is perhaps the most serious. Among others may be mentioned the difficulty of protecting trade creditors in the event of bankruptcy as workers' co-operatives often have few assets of their own—these are usually rented. There is also the possibility that the decision-making process in the co-operative might be slow, and as a result the labour-managed firm might be slow to adopt new methods of production and to experiment with new products. The last two points require elaboration. Unless there is a very strong person running the organisation, major decisions will be made by committees, and experience has shown that in such cases it is difficult to get action. There is no substitute for the entrepreneur, and unless he surfaces at some stage within a co-operative, its days are numbered.

On a somewhat different theme, James Meade (1972) asks "if a firm, as envisaged by Vanek, is compatible with the maintenance of the discipline needed to ensure the efficient operation of a concern which employs a large body of workers". This question implies that workers on their own are not capable of running a large modern business, and if they are not, the business will of necessity have to be a small organisation fighting for its life against capitalistic giants. Furthermore, many people with professional experience of industry are sceptical as to the possibility of combining democratic worker control and efficient management; they say that workers are likely to balk at redundancies or closures even if the health of the enterprise depends on them.

As a counter to these arguments Campbell *et al.* (op. cit.) say that many successes can also be cited, the Mondragon experiment in Spain (to be discussed later) being the best known example. But even here the greatest successes have been with the smaller enterprises. The largest enterprise of the Mondragon group, with over 3,000 workers, has had industrial relations problems and even a strike. It seems therefore that in spite of Meade's doubts about size of business, the advantages gained from industrial peace and harmony in small firms tend to counteract the economies of scale attained in larger firms, associated as the latter generally are, with labour unrest. In any case, there is almost unanimous opinion among co-operative organisers that it is much better to concentrate on building federations of small co-operatives instead of large integrated groups.

Other objections to workers' co-operatives are that workers

do not want to shoulder responsibility for management and this should not be asked of them; most prefer to do their job, take their pay and leave the managers to make the business decisions. Another argument is that the workers do not want their savings tied up with their job so that if the enterprise fails they lose job, savings and all. This, of course, need not happen. Many co-operatives invest their pension funds outside the group, thus ensuring that no worker has all his eggs in one basket. There is also the argument that co-operatives have a tendency to "degenerate" into profit-seeking businesses, indistinguishable from private enterprises. This is usually done by closing off membership, raising the cost of membership to prohibitively high levels or resorting to the devise of taking on hired labour (Blumberg, 1968).

Finally, Professor David O'Mahony is rather sceptical about the whole concept of labour management. In a recent article (O'Mahony, 1979) he says that "in spite of its apparent advantages the labour-managed firm is conspicuous by its absence while the capitalist firm continues to thrive and to constitute the main form of business organisation wherever the market economy prevails". He attributes this to the fact that the establishment of any firm involves the performance of the entrepreneurial functions; that the labour-managed firm is not conducive to the performance of these functions and is not likely to be regarded as a good proposition by workers, other resource supplies or by savers. He then says that the concept of labour management is self contradictory and so is not likely to be chosen by an initiating entrepreneur who wishes to organise the factors of production for the purpose of engaging in business. Accordingly, he says "it looks as if the possibility that labour management could emerge in a market economy as a normal form of business organisation must be ruled out except in special cases".

Despite the shortcomings outlined above and other possible defects, the labour-managed system can, and does, work in certain situations. It is not a system, however, which will develop naturally of its own accord. It is much easier for a person with flair to start his own business and employ labour rather than try to get agreement from a group to pool resources and start a co-operative.

Concluding Observations

In concluding this chapter we quote again from Vanek (1969) who, speaking of labour-managed economies, says that the comparative advantage of these systems becomes even stronger once we leave the strictly economic frame of reference and replace it by one that takes account of broader human values. He says: "Taking a very long view of world events, it seems that if there is a meeting ground for the presently conflicting major world systems and ideologies it is one not too far removed from the labour managed system". There is something in it for both capitalists and communists. Vanek may well be right in this view. A recent article in the *Economist* (3 June 1978) says that it looks as though the British Labour Party has come to the end of the road as far as traditional nationalisation is concerned. Mr Norman Atkinson, treasurer of the Labour Party and a leading figure among the left wing Labour MPs is quoted as saying:

> The whole labour movement should now carefully re-examine its current thinking in regard to managerial concepts. Straight orthodox nationalisation should be replaced by forward looking systems of co-operative self-management.

Mr Atkinson also had especially encouraging words for the Government's Co-operative Development Agency Bill—then before the House of Lords and expected to be enacted shortly afterwards. His only criticism was that the proposed agency would be hopelessly under-financed by a grant of £300,000 a year. Qualified Tory and Liberal support was forthcoming for the Bill, partly because of the essential ideologist ambiguity of co-operative undertakings. As the *Economist* says (*ibid*) "These can be held up either as proxies for an advanced form of socialism or as genuine examples of free enterprise".

Oakeshott (1978) argues, however, that this ambiguity is often used by extremists on both sides of the political spectrum to make a case against co-operatives. He says (p. 245) "to the left, a Mondragon sector" (region in Spain with strong co-operative movement) "is the thin end of the wedge for a capitalist revival; to the right it is the precursor of socialism and workers' power". He continues by saying that even if these arguments do not carry much weight, they do suggest that it may be difficult to recruit support from those on either side of the great class divide with a vested interest in the *status quo*.

Chapter 3

The International Co-operative Alliance and the Movement in Great Britain

The International Co-operative Alliance

The International Co-operative Alliance (ICA) was founded in London in 1895 as an association of national unions of co-operative societies. Its purpose is to propagate co-operative principles and methods and to promote friendly and economic relations between co-operative organisations of all types, both nationally and internationally. Today it comprises organisations in every continent and its total affiliated membership through national organisations exceeds 326 million (see Table 1). Of the total 1976 membership, 2.9 million live in Africa, 46.7 million in USA, 9.5 million in Canada, 4.8 million in Central and Southern America and 3.4 million in Oceania. There are 105.5 million in Asia, of which 68.4 million are in India and 13.3 million in Japan. Europe has 153.1 million members, of which 62.0 million are in the USSR and a further 40.0 million in other centrally planned European economies. The UK has 10.9 million members, France 9.9 million, West Germany 8.7 million, Turkey 3.9 million, Italy 4.1 million and Sweden 3.6 million. The membership given for the Irish Republic is 160,000. This membership does not include agricultural co-operatives or a number of other rural societies which are affiliated to the Irish Co-operative Organisation Society (ICSO).[7] The latter body is not a member of the International Co-operative Alliance

[7] Formerly the Irish Agricultural Organisation Society (IAOS).

(ICA). Irish societies which are members of the International Co-operative Alliance are affiliated to the Irish National Co-operative Council (NCC) with headquarters at 35 Lower Gardiner Street, Dublin. This body caters for such groups as general co-operative stores, public utilities, educational associations, industrial workers' co-operatives, geriatric societies, pharmaceutical distribution, etc. A table showing co-operative membership in Ireland is given in Chapter 7.

The distribution of societies by type of society affiliated to the ICA is given in Table 1. As can be seen from this table the consumer movement, though encompassing only 8.8 per cent of societies, accounts for just under 40 per cent of the total membership. The agricultural co-operatives,

Table 1: *Distribution of world co-operative societies in 1976*

Type of society	*Societies*		*Members*	
	Number	*Per cent of whole*	*Number*	*Per cent of whole*
			'000	
Agricultural	217,530	31.9	63,252	19.4
Consumer	60,248	8.8	124,491	38.2
Credit unions	266,232	39.0	106,693	32.7
Fishery	12,641	1.9	1,862	0.6
Housing	55,350	8.1	11,357	3.5
Productive	41,798	6.1	5,407	1.7
Miscellaneous	29,954	4.2	12,984	4.0
Total	683,753	100.-	326,046	100.-

Source: Review of International Co-operation, Vol. 69, Nos. 3-4, 1976.
Published by International Co-operative Alliance, London.

on the other hand, while accounting for about 32 per cent of the societies, cover less than 20 per cent of the membership. Credit unions are more equal as regards proportions of societies and members. They account for 39 per cent of the former and 33 per cent of the latter. Of the remainder, housing co-operatives are the most important. The 55,000 of these cover 8 per cent of the societies and 3.5 per cent or 11.4 million members. Productive, or workers' co-operatives cover 6 per cent of the societies and 1.7 per cent or 5.4 million members. Fishery and miscellaneous societies make up the balance. The fishery co-operatives cover only 1.9 per cent of the societies and 0.6 per cent of the membership.

The figures for co-operative membership must be taken with some caution. In many cases people are members in name only. This is particularly true of agricultural co-operatives where farmers are members by virtue of their having bought shares at some time but give little continuing support to the co-operative. Membership figures are also confusing because one person can be a member of several co-operatives.

Workers' Co-operatives in Britain

The modern formal British co-operative movement dates from 1844 when 28 poor weavers of Rochdale in Britain came together with a capital of £1 each to open a small retail shop. They adopted a set of rules, which were later to become enshrined as the Rochdale Principles and which today effectively guide the philosophy and conduct of co-operative societies all over the world (Bolger, 1977). At the start it was an open question whether the co-operative movement in Britain would go producer or consumer. As it turned out, consumer co-operatives have proved the most powerful. The emphasis derives, to a major extent, from the influence of Beatrice and Sydney Webb (1921) who carried on a life-long attack on producer co-operation and were very strong and effective advocates of consumer co-operation. They advocated collective bargaining and collectivism which made a negative attitude to producer co-operatives inevitable (Webb, 1921). Availability of capital was another factor which favoured the consumer orientation. Turnover of capital is much slower in production than in trade. Hence if a group is short of capital, trading is more easily organised than production.

Despite criticisms from many sources, however, both producer and consumer co-operatives grew rapidly in the early years of the movement. By 1863 there were 454 such societies in existence in Britain. The first major blow for the producer co-operatives came in 1870 when the movement was shaken by the failure of a number of societies, mainly in textiles, coal mining and engineering. Nevertheless, the thirty-year period from 1874 to 1905 was one of considerable expansion for the producer co-operative movement. The number of firms (excluding agricultural co-operatives) increased from 15 in 1874 to 109 in 1905 but from then onwards they steadily declined to 48 in 1945 and to about 19 in 1977. The latter does not include the government co-operative, Meriden, which is the best known but least representative of all worker co-operatives, having been established with government support, after a determined fight by workers to resist factory closure. Neither do they include what are known as the ICOM (common ownership) group, i.e., firms which have changed over from private enterprise to co-operatives in recent years and others which have started from scratch using ICOM model rules. The latter are not registered under the Industrial and Provident Societies' Acts, and are therefore difficult to enumerate from official sources. We understand, however, that there are now over 300 such enterprises in Britain. (L. Stettner, Personal Communication, March 1980).

Most of the older co-operatives are concentrated in the footwear, textiles and printing industries and a few of these have put up a remarkable survival record matched by few private capitalistic concerns (see Table 2).

Table 2: *List of surviving older style producers' co-operatives registered under the UK Industrial and Provident Societies' Acts in 1977.*[a]

Name	*Date of registration*	*Sales, 1977*	*Number of employees*
		£	
Printers			
Leicester Printers Ltd.	1892	683,655	89
Nottingham Printers Ltd.	1895	139,271	15
Derby Printers Ltd.	1899	147,160	26
Bristol Printers Ltd.[b]	1909	14,086	9
Blackfriars Press Ltd., Leicester	1914	694,035	89
Watford Printers Ltd., Herts.	1921	370,267	53
Footwear manufacture			
NPS Shoes Ltd., Wollaston	1881	685,501	68
Equity Shoes Ltd., Leicester	1887	1,912,996	204
St. Crispen Footwear Ltd., Wellingborough	1891	570,919	92
Avalon Footwear Ltd., Kettering	1892	820,590	111
Clothing manufacture			
Queen Eleanor Ltd., Kettering	1897	485,058	94
Ideal Clothiers Ltd., Wellingborough	1900	1,720,311	540
Sunray Textiles Ltd., Coalville	1934	321,596	70
Miscellaneous			
Wallsall Locks Ltd.	1874	877,144	161
Leicester Carriage Builders Ltd.	1903	319,475	45
Co-operative London's Cabmen's Association	1908	–	–
Metropolitan Motor Cab Co-operative, London	1927	–	–
Co-operative Planning Ltd., London	1946	–	–
SBD Co-operative Association Ltd.	1974	–	–
Total		9,762,064	1,666

(a) This list does not include The British Co-operative Bank with headquarters in Manchester, which is discussed on page

(b) Wound up in 1977.

Source: Registry of Friendly Societies, 17 North Audley Street, London W1Y 2AP

At the present time the producer co-operative sector in Britain is essentially divided into three groupings:

1. The older style producer co-operatives, a few of which have survived from the pioneer days and some new ones formed recently.
2. The grouping of common ownership enterprises known

as ICOM (Industrial Common Ownership Movement), and

3. The worker take-overs promoted by Mr. A. Benn who was Secretary for Industry in the early 1970s.

Old Style Producers' Co-operatives

The names, year of establishment, sales and numbers employed in the 19 surviving older style co-operatives in 1977 are shown in Table 2. As can be seen from this table the turnover of these co-operatives in 1977 was £9.8 million with a total labour force of 1,666 people. Though structures vary from enterprise to enterprise, ownership is basically vested in the "members" of the co-operatives who may include some or all of the workforce, retired workers, or their families, outside well-wishers and institutions such as trade unions or wholesale consumer co-operatives. Membership involves the ownership of a (usually) nominal number of shares, and the principle of one man one vote rules. Capital is rewarded at fixed rates of interest and shares remain at their nominal value. Most co-operatives pay part of any surplus to workers in proportion to their wages during the year and part to other members. There is seldom any restriction on pay differentials.

Generally, workers' (producers') co-operatives in the UK are registered under the Industrial and Provident Societies' Acts. The principal act is the Industrial and Provident Societies' Act, 1965, Section I of which states that for an enterprise to be registered under the Act it must, except in special circumstances, be a bona fide co-operative society. The Act is administered by the Registrar of Friendly Societies and he has some discretion as to what constitutes a bona fide co-operative. No statutory definition of a bona fide co-operative is laid down but it is expected that it satisfy certain conditions, such as:

(a) The business of the society will be conducted for

the mutual benefit of its members, in such a way that the benefit which members obtain will, in the main, stem from their participation in the business;

(b) Control of the society will be vested in the members equally and not in accordance with financial interest in the society—i.e., one man one vote;

(c) Interest payable on share and loan capital will not exceed the rate needed to obtain and retain the capital required to carry out the objects of the society. A society which carries on business mainly for the payment of interest, dividends or bonuses on money invested with the society is not a bona fide co-operative;

(d) The profits of the society's business after payment of interest on share capital if distributable among its members will, under the rules, be distributed in proportion to the extent they have traded with or taken part in the business of the society;

(e) There shall be no artificial restriction of membership with the object of increasing proprietary rights and interests. There may, of course, be grounds for restricting membership that do not offend the co-operative principle: for example, the membership of a club might be limited by the size of the premises, the membership of a workers' co-operative could be limited to the number of workers required for its successful operation.

Other conditions of registration are:

(f) The society must have at least seven members.

(g) The rules of the society must provide for all matters required by Section I of the Act, and

(h) the proposed name of the society must not be undesirable.

The Common Ownership Movement

The Common Ownership Movement has evolved from the initiative of Ernest Bader. In 1951 he and his family gave over 90 per cent of their shares in Scott Bader and Co. (manufacturers of chemicals and plastics) to a commonwealth or trust comprising all their employees. The final 10 per cent was purchased by the employees in 1963. A proportion of the trust's profits are committed by deed to the promotion of similar worker-owned enterprises. In 1958 Bader formed the Society of Democratic Integration in Industry to further promote his ideas and in 1971 its name was changed to the Industrial Common Ownership Movement (ICOM). A further development was the passing of the Industrial Common Ownership Act in 1976 for the purpose of giving financial assistance to such co-operatives.

At present there are 18 full member companies of ICOM. The Scott Bader enterprise is still the largest with a labour force of around 430 and an annual turnover of around £15 million. It is followed by Bewley's Cafes of Dublin which were similarly converted from family to worker-ownership in 1972. This group (which is described in more detail later) has 400 employees. The remainder are mostly small firms.

In 1973 an organisation, The Industrial Common Ownership Finance Ltd. (ICOF) was formed to provide loan capital to common ownership enterprises. It has a Board of trustees drawn from ICOM members. ICOF has received loans from a number of individuals who are sympathetic to the idea of common ownership. Under the Industrial Common Ownership Act, ICOF also has access to a government loan fund of £250,000 for lending to common ownership and co-operative enterprises.

The essential difference between ICOM firms and the older producer co-operatives is that the former have a membership open only to the workers in the business, although there are three different structures. The most common is for all the shares in the company to be owned by a holding company which is limited by guarantee and democratically controlled by a membership which is restricted to the members of the operating company. This structure presents the easiest way for an existing private company to convert to common ownership.

Another option for a newly-created company is to be limited by guarantee, with no share capital, based entirely on loan stock. An alternative is to be limited by shares, with all shares issued to employees, and votes normally being proportional to the shares held. The latter would conflict with the requirements of most co-operatives and with the ICOM model rules which specify that everybody must have an equal say.

The constitution of many ICOM firms define the decision-making process, maximum wage differentials and even a maximum size for a firm. All firms adopt the principle of collective ownership as opposed to Mondragon's principle of individual ownership. Collective ownership means that the company's assets are owned by the entire workforce as a group, and as a group which changes with time. No individual has the right to draw on or enjoy a personal share of the assets and he receives no pay-out (except the lump sum which is part of his pension rights) when he leaves.

Government Co-operatives

The worker take-overs promoted by Mr Benn have attracted much more publicity than the other groupings of producer co-operatives. There were originally three firms involved in these take-overs, the Scottish Daily News in Glasgow, Meriden (a motor bicycle manufacturing company near Coventry) and Kirkby Manufacturing and Engineering (KME) outside Liverpool. They were all converted to co-operatives for the same reason; their capitalist owner had found them non-viable and proposed closing them down. The conversion was made possible by a substantial injection of government money. KME received nearly £4 million as a grant from the government in 1975 while in April 1977 it got a further £86,000. In 1975 Meriden received a government grant of £0.75 million and a 15-year loan of £4.2 million to purchase the factory and run it as a co-operative. About the same time the government advanced £1.2 million to Scottish News Enterprises Ltd., to enable it to acquire premises previously used by the Scottish Daily Express and publish a new daily newspaper, The Scottish Daily News. In each case independent consultants said that the enterprise had little prospects of becoming financially viable and according to Campbell and Foster (1974, p. 13) the decision to back them was forced through the Cabinet by Mr Benn (Bruce-Gardyne, 1978).

The Scottish Daily News was the first casualty. This was because of the general difficulties being faced by the newspaper industry, as well as internal strife in the enterprise. Meanwhile, Meriden and KME survived. In the first year of operation as a co-operative (1975/76) KME recorded a £1.5 million loss (McKay and Barr, 1976). In the following 18 months production increased by over 50 per cent with only a marginal increase in the labour force (from 750 to about 800 workers) and in 1977 it made a small profit.

In 1978 it faced new difficulties and PA Management Consultants were called in to make recommendations. Their report mapped out a prosperous future for the venture if certain changes were introduced. These included the hiring of marketing specialists, the strengthening of the general commercial management expertise, the boosting of productivity and the implementation of a rationalisation programme, which meant abandoning the production of fruit drinks and night storage heaters and concentrating instead on the main business, of making central heating radiators, air conditioning equipment and metal presswork. It also recommended an urgent injection of £2.9 million in capital over a period of three years. The rationalisation programme was adopted but the other suggestions were not put into operation. In particular, the Cabinet rejected the plea for extra capital on the grounds that it had already contributed £4.8 million since 1974. The Department of Industry announced however, that temporary aid of £150,000 would be made available immediately to keep the firm going until such a time as a working party chaired by Mr Douglas Hague made recommendations on the future of the co-operative. This report published on the 16 November 1978 recommended that the best way of saving jobs at the factory was to allow the co-operative to be taken over by a private engineering company. At one stage it was announced that the firm was to be taken over by Worcester Engineering Company but this company refused to go ahead with the take over. It is claimed that this refusal was due to resistance from the work-force. At the time of writing (December 1979) a liquidator had been appointed to wind up the co-operative.

Meriden is also in a difficult position. Its debts were very much higher than those of KME at the time the latter became a co-operative. At KME there was no interruption of production at take-over and an outright grant of £3.9 million made it possible for production to be carried on in spite of the liquidation of a subsidiary company. At Meriden, on the other hand, the workers had to occupy the factory for 18 months before it was turned into a co-operative and as a result of this long siege they were not in a position to provide any of the share capital themselves. Despite this the government gave a grant of £0.75 million only, while the balance was made available in the form of a 15-year government loan of £4.2 million. The grant and loan combined had to be less than £5 million to come within the terms of the Industry Act of 1972 but because the grant was so small the co-operative was launched in April 1975 with nearly all its capital in the form of a repayable loan. In the first year of operation as a co-operative, Meriden made a loss of £1.2 million but its position has improved since then. In 1977 Sir Arnold Weinstock of GEC provided a credit facility of

£1 million and also put in managers from his own firm to help overcome the financial and marketing problems Meriden was facing. Another firm, GKN, had earlier provided managerial help. At the beginning of 1978 the number of workers had increased to about 600 from about 350 in April 1975. Production at the latter date was about 300 machines a week. It is now felt that the enterprise may be able to survive because it has large orders for its motorbikes.

The experience at Meriden is of much interest to our discussion. When it was started all workers, with the exception of five top executives, were paid at the same rate. Also there was no job demarcation. If people were needed to move from one job to another to overcome a bottleneck they moved. Wages at Meriden, however, were, and are, substantially below those at local concerns but early in 1978 a self-financing bonus scheme was introduced to alter this situation. Under this scheme all workers got a bonus for increased production but 250 workers identified as skilled received upwards of around £4 per week more than the other 400 members. The bonus has been related to the achievement of output targets.

The introduction of differentials into the co-operative marked a fairly radical change and gave rise to heated debate within Meriden. The Chairman, Mr John Rosamund, said that the main problem was to recruit sufficient skilled workers because the co-operative wages have fallen out of line with prevailing Coventry rates. Many members had been forced to request help in the form of family income supplements (Smith, 1978).

Despite many innovations no one at Meriden is yet prepared to make bold claims about long-term prospects. The pressure on the co-operative is not just to become economically viable. Its formation, which followed an 18 months sit-in by the workforce, was heralded as a major social experiment. The leading figure during that occupation, Mr Dennis Johnson, believes the co-operative has now strayed from its original ideals. After steering Meriden through the difficult first three years he resigned as Chairman in September 1977 and left the factory where he had worked since he was a teenager, retiring to his trade as a fitter with Jaguar of Coventry.

His departure came a few weeks after it was decided to appoint a new managing director to complete the co-operative's team of five senior executives. At the time of his resignation, Mr Johnson blamed the pressure of the job, but a more important factor was the move towards what he described as conventional management. Smith (1978) quotes him as saying "To me the idea of employing full-time executives at £10,000 a year, plus a car, plus expenses is a total contradiction of what we were aiming for at Meriden". Mr Johnson believes that the workers will now become less involved in the decision-making process and that a "them and us" mentality will again develop.

In the original appeal for state aid in April 1974, the need for capable professional management was fully accepted by the co-operative. But there were those like Johnson who argued that management could be promoted from within the organisation. After many vicissitudes, however, it became clear to a majority of workers that professionals would have to be called in, and though the debate continues it seems likely that they are there to stay.

The Cumbrian Industrial Co-operative Experiment

The industrial co-operative experiment was one project in a larger Cumbrian Community Development Programme (CDP). The latter in turn was part of a national action and research experiment operating in twelve small areas in the UK. Launched in 1969 by the Home Office as part of the British poverty programme the projects aimed to focus in depth on the fundamental problems of the areas in which they were located, with a view to understanding these problems and their causes and aiming to initiate action programmes to test out ways of solving them. A primary purpose was that of local community involvement, both in defining problems and taking action (Pearse, 1977). We select the Cumbrian experiment for examination because it was the first project to employ a wholetime industrial co-operative officer and because it shows up starkly some of the problems encountered in organising industrial co-operatives.

West Cumbria has traditionally been a special problem area as far as government regional policies are concerned. Since 1927 unemployment has been at least twice the national average and often much worse. Successive regional policies have done little to improve matters; they have been able to do no more than maintain the *status quo*. The Cumbria Development Project (CDP) was established in May 1972 by the Cumberland Co. Council at the invitation of the Home Office. The project has consisted of an action and research team, the former employed by the Co. Council, the latter by the Department of Social Administration and Social Work at the University of York. The project was expected to function for a five-year term during which the Home Office would meet 100 per cent of the research costs and 75 per cent of the action costs. The Co. Council would contribute the remaining quarter.

From its initiation the Cumbrian Project had been involved with many facets of community life: an information and action centre in Cleator Moor; a mobile information service, support and servicing of local community action groups, investigation of the needs of the elderly, adventure playgrounds and youth projects, research into transport problems and housing issues and tenant co-operative housing associations. Despite all these projects, however, the central substantive problems of the area remained—high unemployment, lack of opportunities and low levels of investment.

In an effort to overcome this problem, discussions were held with a consultant, with a view to the development of industrial co-operatives in the area. The consultant reported in June 1974 that viable jobs could be created in the Cumbrian area and that the establishment of industrial co-operatives was a worthwhile method of creating jobs locally. In order to do this, however, the appointment of an Industrial Officer for Common Ownership Projects would be necessary. The functions of the officer would be to stimulate the growth and development of indigenous enterprises and carry out investigations into the concept of a community workshop or entrepreneurial seed bed which could provide a sheltered base for co-operatives in their early stages of formation.

The proposed appointment was agreed by the CDP Management Committee which referred the whole scheme to the Cumbria County's Personnel Sub-Committee. This Committee approved the post, but only on the casting vote of the Chairman. This close decision did not bode well for the future of the project.

The industrial co-operative officer was appointed in early 1975, but even before taking up his appointment Pearse (1977, p. 10) reports that political clouds had begun to assemble. The first setback came when the Co. Council's Management Committee refused to confirm a decision made by its Chairman and Vice Chairman to lease at £5 per week a set of offices, storage rooms and a yard in Whitehaven as a potential base for a community workshop. This decision had serious implications for the whole project. In setting up the workshop it was intended to provide in one place, plant, machinery and selected manufacturing skills which could be leased to those wanting to test out the technical and economic possibilities of their ideas. Also the workshop could become the springboard for proven ideas for the development of industrial co-operatives. It was envisaged that the Industrial Co-operative Officer would supervise this workshop with the help of a foreman. But this never came to pass.

On taking up appointment the Industrial Co-operative Officer set about familiarising himself with the job and working out specifications for suitable projects. The most ambitious of these was what became known as the Clemcote project.

This was a small structural engineering project which would employ ten men from the region, who were already working outside the area on similar work. None of the men, however, had capital to invest in the project.

A feasibility study showed that the project would be viable, but in order to get it underway £25,000 would be needed. Since West Cumbria was a special development area it was expected that the Department of Industry would offer finance on a "matching" basis so that only £12,500 would have to be found locally. Those involved with the experiment expected that this amount could be found easily, that the County Council would be prepared to put up most of the finance. No such backing was, however, forthcoming. The reaction from the County Council Finance Department was that such backing was not desirable and would create a dangerous precedent in the industrial field. It was obvious therefore that funds would have to be found elsewhere.

Thus began a round of discussions with various financial establishments, banks, finance houses, charitable trusts and so forth but the immediate reaction from all these establishments was completely negative. Even the manager of the Co-operative Bank in Newcastle-upon-Tyne was not prepared to support the experiment. He suggested that the "time was not right" for such ventures; and that the record of previous co-operatives did little to merit requests of this sort. At this stage the whole future of the project seemed to be in grave doubt.

However, in February 1976 Industrial Common Ownership Finance Ltd., the financial wing of the ICOM movement indicated that they would consider the possibility of a £10,500 loan for Clemcote, subject to the company becoming a bona fide common ownership company. This was agreed and with £10,500 in hand an approach was made to the Department of Industry for another £10,500 matching money and for an additional £4,000 in Special Development Area Grants. Unfortunately, all these applications were turned down without any reason being given. As a result the project has had to be shelved.

Another project—a building co-operative—suffered the same fate. Though appearing feasible, no money could be found to buy the necessary machinery required. There was also a broad suggestion from the CDP Management Committee that the launching of a building co-operative was not particularly desirable anyhow, and one got the impression that the elected County Councillors were not particularly enamoured with publically funded co-operatives which were likely to compete with established private businesses.

When it became clear that sources of risk capital for the launching of co-operatives were going to be hard to find, thought was given to the setting up of a special revolving fund to make loans and grants to new common ownership enterprises. The plans for the fund envisaged seeking initial grants from the County Council, District and Parish Council as well as donations or low interest loans from private sources. The target set was £10,000 to £20,000 in the first year. This was a small sum but it would have enabled a number of enterprises to be funded. Regrettably, however, the scheme never got off the ground, a political controversy over the whole Community Development Project erupted in the County Council and led to the closure of the project in March 1976, one year before it was due to end.

After the closure of the CDP the County Council agreed to continue having the Industrial Officer in post for the remainder of his three year contract, but now reporting direct to the Council's Economic Development Committee. The title of the post was also changed to that of Small Business Advisory Officer, with the emphasis placed on the creation of jobs in private enterprises rather than in co-operatives. The officer has been given new offices in Whitehaven where they were denied to him in his previous role.

It is difficult for us to draw objective conclusions from this experiment. We must rely mainly on written comments and most of these are anything but impartial. It would appear, however, that there were ideological conflicts within the County Council from the start, and these did not help, particularly when it came to getting funds for enterprises. As can be seen, shortage of finance was the immediate cause of failure which again goes to show the importance of finance in this area and the need for some specific funding source, such as a co-operative bank, a community fund, or some other sympathetic lender.

The British Co-operative Bank[8]

Though this bank is not a workers' co-operative it is of some interest to describe its history since it is now about to play a positive role in funding such co-operatives. The Co-operative Bank was established in 1872 under the title of Loan and Deposit Department of the Co-operative Wholesale Society Ltd., (CWS). This society had been incorporated nine years earlier in 1863 to supply the requirements of co-operative retail societies throughout the country. On foundation, the Loan and Deposit Department of the CWS could not be called a bank because of a legal disability dating from 1862 which prevented the formation of banks by co-operative societies. This legal disability was removed in 1876 and thereafter the title CWS Bank became better known.

At the outset progress by the bank was slow. In 1882 total assets were only £214,000, in 1892, £605,000 and in 1902, £1,692,000. There were only a few hundred current accounts held in 1907. In 1912 a campaign was inaugurated with great success to obtain trade union accounts and today the majority of trade unions in the country bank with the Co-operative Bank. In 1919 the number of current accounts had risen to 5,300 and total assets exceeded £10 million.

The following years were marked by further expansion.

[8]For a more detailed account see "A Brief History of the Co-operative Bank, 1872-1972" in *Co-operative Bank Ltd*, Centenary Issue, 1972, P.O. Box 101, New Century House, Manchester, M6O 4EP.

Between 1920 and 1922 the first branches of the bank were opened in London, Newcastle-upon-Tyne and Bristol, while retail Co-operative Societies began to act as agents of the bank for the acceptance of deposits and the encashment of cheques. This development attracted a much wider clientele than heretofore and business grew accordingly.

In those years also the bank began to develop an overseas business. Associations were formed with Russian Co-operatives for the importing of grain and other commodities and with other organisations for the financing of certain Australian Co-operative wheat pools and New Zealand dairy produce. At the same time, links with co-operative banks abroad were being forged through membership of the International Co-operative Alliance Banking Committee which met for the first time in 1922 at Basle, Switzerland.

By 1929 the number of current accounts in the CWS bank had risen to 26,000 and total assets to £43 million. The year 1930 was marked by the opening of the new head office building of the bank in Manchester where it has since remained.

The outbreak of war in 1939 brought some problems, but after the cessation of hostilities in 1945 the bank once more set out on a course of steady expansion. Between 1946 and 1951 over 100 Local Authority Councils transferred their accounts to it and to meet these demands new branches were opened in Birmingham, Cardiff, Chemsford, Derby, Durham, Grimsby, Leeds, Newport, Northampton, Nottingham, Sheffield, Stafford and Stoke-on-Trent, a truly national network of banks was therefore being developed.

The bank continued its steady development throughout the 1950s and 1960s. In 1969 it formed an entirely new subsidiary company "Co-operative Commercial Bank Ltd" which operates from the City of London in the important Euro-currency and inter-bank markets. This bank has now become well established and has formed very firm ties with a number of banks in Europe and elsewhere.

Meanwhile the Co-operative Bank has itself embarked on

a new phase of branch extension and development. Several new branches have been opened with the object of ringing the greater London area at strategic points. In addition several other branches have been opened in important provincial cities and towns.

The year 1971 saw the culmination of a century of co-operative banking in England with the passing of the Co-operative Bank Act of that year. By means of a Parliamentary Bill the Bank was separated from the parent organisation and registered under the Companies' Acts as Co-operative Bank Ltd. The newly formed bank remains, however, a wholly owned subsidiary of the CWS but its revised constitution has enhanced its status in the banking world. So after more than a century the wheel has turned full circle. Parliament in 1862 had barred Co-operative Societies from banking; Parliament in 1971 formally gave its imprimatur to the Co-operative Bank as a separate part of the British Banking system.

In its new guise the Co-operative Bank became a member of the British Bankers Association in 1972. It took a little longer to be admitted to the Bankers' Clearing House in Lombard Street. For most of its existence, CWS clearing had been carried out on agency by one of the joint stock banks. The change came in February 1974 when the Co-operative Bank Ltd., was accepted as a Clearing Bank in its own right, the first new member to be admitted to the Clearing House since 1936. Direct participation in the clearing operations began in 1975.

Both before, and since, its incorporation as a recognised financial institution, the Co-operative Bank has introduced a number of new initiatives. It was the first bank (December 1973) to offer commission free banking for current account customers who maintained their accounts in credit. Other banks now offer this concession but only if a substantial credit balance is maintained. Interest at one half per cent, calculated daily, is also paid by the Co-operative Bank on current account balances. The CWS pioneered this practice many years ago and the Co-operative Bank is still the only one to carry it on.

Other services include a Co-operative Barclaycard through the Barclaycard scheme and its own Euro-Cheque Card usable in some 13,000 bank branches in Britain as well as in most banks in Europe and in retail outlets. Recently it has also launched a credit card for people who have no bank account. This is called Handycard, a budget account card. To obtain a card customers make a regular payment of say £10 a month and enjoy a credit limit of 24 times the monthly payment. Almost 80 per cent of Handycard applicants declare that they do not have a bank account.

Another compelling attraction to new customers is convenience. Through the use of co-operative stores, for basic banking transactions, the Co-operative Bank has more locations in the UK for cashing cheques and making deposits than any other bank. Most of these facilities are open for longer hours and on more days than any other bank also. Approximately 4,000 co-operative shops and stores provide "Cash a Cheque" facility known as the "Handybank" scheme.

Another innovation by the Co-operative Bank has been a recent scheme to finance workers' co-operatives. Announcing the scheme in July 1978, Sir Arthur Sudgen, Chairman, said that the bank was prepared, if necessary, to match pound for pound the joint investment of members of new worker co-operatives with loans on basic conditions which are designed to ensure total involvement of workers in the firm. By the latter he meant that "the financial commitment of the members would be such as to represent 'a meaningful sum' for each person." He also stated that the terms of the loans will be better than those given by other lending institutions for new business ventures (Spencer, 1978).

This is the first time that the bank has shown much interest in the workers' movement. It now seems that this policy is to be reversed but whether workers will take up the offer is another matter. What is required next is a drive to get people interested in establishing workers' co-operatives. When this happens the availability of funds will prove very useful. At one stage there were rumours that the Co-operative Bank was interested in setting up branches in the Irish Republic, both for general business and for the funding of workers' co-operatives. Recent events relating to EMS have, however, created difficulties in this regard and the matter has had to be deferred for the time being.*

Current Developments

Industrial Common Ownership Act

Co-operation in Britain has been given an added impetus recently by a number of measures, most prominent of which is the Industrial Common Ownership Act 1976, sponsored by David Watkins, M.P. The Act aims to provide financial assistance to productive enterprises which subscribe to co-operative principles. Conditions under which an enterprise may be recognised as subscribing to such principles and, hence, be in a position to avail of this aid are laid down in the Act. Up to £30,000 per annum for five years from 1976 can be given as a grant to any relevant body for the purpose of assisting that body to provide advice about the organisation of common ownership and co-operative enterprises. Grants and loans, up to a total of £250,000, can also be given over the five years from 1976 to a relevant body for the purpose of assisting that body to make loans to common ownership and co-operative enterprises. Examples of bodies who are availing of this assistance are the Industrial Common Ownership Movement, Industrial Common Ownership Finance Ltd., and the Scottish Co-operatives' Development Committee. The Act does not apply in Northern Ireland.

*Brierley, Ian, Personal Communication, 19 December, 1978.

The Scottish Co-operative Development Committee (SCDC)

This is an independent body set up to encourage the growth of workers' co-operatives in Scotland. It was started two years ago and in June 1977 was recognised by the Government as an official body under the Industrial Common Ownership Act and last year received an £8,000 grant from the Department of Industry. It employs a full-time Development Officer, Mr. Cairns Campbell.

Two years ago there were five workers' co-operatives in Scotland; now there are sixteen. Most are very small and in total they employ less than 200 persons. Only four or five co-operatives are in the manufacturing sector.

The SCDC's priority has been the encouragement of new manufacturing co-operatives through:

(a) converting existing businesses, and
(b) starting new co-operatives.

In setting out to achieve these objectives informal discussions were held with a number of businesses about the possibilities of conversions and a press advertisement produced a further limited response. At the same time, the Committee placed a series of articles in journals circulating in the business community to alert solicitors, the owners of small companies, etc., to the possibilities of co-operative enterprise. It may, however, be some time before the seeds sown bear fruit. In the meantime, a research project on whether small businesses about to close down are suitable for conversion to co-operatives awaits finance. Shortage of funds for administrative and developmental work is the main constraint at present. The grant of £8,000 is entirely inadequate.

Co-operative Development Agency

In 1978 the Co-operative Development Agency Act was passed. This Act seeks to implement the recommendations embodied in the majority report of a Working Group set up to determine the type of agency which would best further the interests of the co-operative movement generally. The Agency set up under the Act will attempt to fulfil its objectives by working with existing co-operative organisations to co-ordinate and facilitate the development of co-operative activities. The main role of the Agency will be advisory and promotional—giving guidance to co-operatives, appraising and evaluating projects, undertaking research and generally encouraging the development of successful co-operatives. A grant of £300,000 per annum is being made available to finance the workings of the Agency over the next three years. The Co-operative Development Agency has been criticised on the grounds that it will not be directly involved in establishing co-operatives or in financing co-operative development.

Since the passing of the Act, the British Co-operative Bank has launched the scheme, outlined above, to aid worker co-operatives, by providing up to half the initial cash required to establish a society. Government finance for co-operatives is also available under the Job Creation Programme (JCP) and many of the new co-operatives have been set up with JCP money. The scheme is short term, however, and projects must become self-sufficient within a year. It remains to be seen therefore how many JCP founded co-operatives will survive the ending of JCP finance.

Another legal aid to co-operatives was contained in the 1976 Finance Act which gave exemption from capital gains and capital transfer tax to companies which are converting to a co-operative structure. Other developments include tentative steps by Wandsworth Local Council to assist the development of co-operatives in its area.

The Action Resource Centre

Since co-operatives and community projects very often fail because of inexpert management, some means of providing such groups with skilled managers is essential. The Action Resource Centre in the UK has come into existence for this purpose. It was founded in London in 1973 on the initiative of a small group of public-spirited businessmen from major companies who felt that the provision of expert advice and guidance to developing groups was very often more useful than cash donations. To provide such advice the centre, in co-operation with a number of private firms, arranges for secondment of skilled manpower to assist community and other projects designed to combat unemployment. It also provides regular advisory help to such projects in the areas of finance, administration, marketing, training, design, etc.

Many of the schemes the Resource Action Centre is backing through secondment, are new enterprises which will broaden the base of permanent jobs in communities. Indeed before it moves in, the centre will need evidence that an initiative it assists will go some way towards achieving this objective. The benefits of well matched secondments are mutual. A project gains expertise it could not initially afford to purchase while the secondee gains the invaluable experience of testing and increasing his/her skills in an alternative environment. A company gains from the increased experience and broadened approach of personnel who have been on secondment. Secondment may, therefore, be viewed as a particularly relevant part of a person's training programme or as a re-vitalising time out in mid-career or later life.

How to translate approval of the principle of secondment into practice is not always easy. The first step is to appoint a company linkman who liaises with the Action Resource Centre in order to match personnel available to requirements. This is sometimes difficult and the Action Resource Centre's role as broker has to be flexible to meet the requirements of different companies, some of whom can only release personnel for a few hours each month, while others may be able to second a person for two or even three years.

Most of the Action Resource Centre's income is donated by industrial and commercial companies (there are now 113 subscribers) with further support from the Home Office and individuals. In 1977/78 a sum of £40,000 was needed to cover budgeted expenditure. This includes the salaries of five permanent staff and other administrative expenditure.

Examples of the type of projects which have been aided by the Action Resource Centre are:

1. The secondment for one year of a manager from Rank Xerox to a co-operative engaged in the manufacture of children's toys. He had the job of setting up the business and was responsible for finance, production and marketing, as well as establishing links with government agencies and local business. British Petroleum also seconded a finance manager for two days a week to the same co-operative. This co-operative was set up with a grant of £70,000 from the Manpower Services Commission and donations of £12,500 from private enterprises.

2. A second project in which the Action Resource Centre was involved was in Islington where 20 small firms were about to lose their premises. To help ensure an orderly transfer of the firms to new locations the Action Resource Centre got the Commercial Finance Corporation to survey the 20 firms involved. The results of this survey will help the Centre to decide how best to deploy its resources to help in the most effective way.

3. A marketing manager from ESSO acted as a deputy manager for a transitional employment programme for young people under the care of the Inner London Probation and Aftercare Service. His business expertise was used to set up a contracting company to find work and to draw up contracts for the employees. Later McAlpines seconded a building manager to work with the team for three days a week, arranging contracts and supervising work on site. A leaflet from the Action Resource Centre at 4 Cromwell Place, London, gives a long list of other projects which are being aided.

Recent Survey of Small British Co-operatives

In their Report (referred to above) Chaplin and Cowe describe the results of a survey of small British co-operatives which they carried out in 1977. The aim of this survey was to:

(a) Identify types, history, strengths, weaknesses and performance of worker co-operatives in Britain.
(b) Attempt to discern aspects of co-operatives that appeared to be crucial in their medium-term viability and thus to be able to suggest ways in which groups contemplating the establishment of new co-operatives could minimise the chance of failure in the short-run; and
(c) make recommendations as to the needs for support, co-ordination and sharing of resources among both operating and planned co-operatives.

The study was limited from the outset to manufacturing and service enterprises, explicitly excluding consumer and agricultural co-operatives. It was decided to concentrate on small co-operatives having less than 200 workers, partly because the authors were interested in small businesses and, partly because most new co-operatives start small. The results are based on a postal questionnaire supplemented by in-depth analysis of a few groups in the Manchester area.

The Sample

Forty-two existing co-operatives and 15 planned co-operatives were approached. Completed questionnaires were received from 30 of these, 24 existing co-operatives and six planned ventures. Three of the existing co-operatives were businesses which had changed from private to common ownership, while the remainder had originated as co-operatives under either old style or ICOM rules. The nature of the businesses of the operating and planned co-operatives in the sample was as follows.

	Operating	Planned
Food production and sale	8	-
Manufacturing (general)	5	4
Scientific manufacture/service	2	1
Books/publishing/printing	4	-
Crafts	2	-
Ecology	1	-
Clothing	1	-
Miscellaneous repairs	1	1
Total	24	6

Size of Business

The average number of full-time workers in the existing co-operatives in the sample was nine. None had more than 40 workers and 14 had under 10. Many employ part-time workers and in five cases the number of part-timers was at least equal to the number of whole-timers. Many of the groups were assisted by voluntary workers of one kind or another while in three cases there were no paid workers at all.

The average turnover (total sales) of the sample was about £100,000 per annum but this figure was exaggerated by a few companies which had over £¼ million turnover. The majority had sales of less than £40,000 per annum.

The planned co-operatives expect to employ an average of 19 whole-time workers and their expected turnover is an average of £24,000 per annum.

Origins

The average age of the co-operatives surveyed was four years, but this includes significant variations. Seventeen had commenced operations in 1972 while the oldest two groups were started in 1964 and 1965. The time between the original idea to set up a co-operative and the actual commencement of operations was about two years; this includes three (all in 1976) which only took one or two months and three which took five years.

Very diverse ideas were given as to the reasons for setting up or planning to set up co-operatives. Only one firm from each group gave closure of existing plant as the reason. In every case with the planned co-operative, at least part of the idea came from the need to provide employment and the availability of some government finance for this purpose. The need to provide employment was mentioned by only nine of the existing co-operatives. Seven mentioned the need to create a fairer employment situation and four mentioned the promotion of a better society as a whole as the reason for setting up.

Problems

The major problems experienced by the operating co-operatives in setting up business are not significantly different from those encountered by any new business, especially a small business. The aspects mentioned most frequently were finance and premises. In nine cases finance was the main problem and in seven cases it was premises. In very few cases was the finding of a suitable product a problem.

With regard to problems experienced since starting, people and organisational problems were those mentioned most frequently. The co-operative aspects of the enterprise seem to have an increasing significance here. In 14 cases some aspects of internal organisation was mentioned as having been a major problem since the co-operative started, with personality clashes being mentioned three times. Finance continued to be a major problem for many enterprises, but finding sales outlets and finding people willing to join the co-operative had, in general, become more important. The latter was mentioned on six occasions as being likely to cause major problems in future. It would appear from these replies that the operators had under-estimated the difficulties of running a co-operative organisation.

Financial Resources

The pattern of finance for the co-operatives in the sample is similar to that for most small businesses. Personal savings provided initial funds for over half the established co-operatives, while one-third obtained finance from commercial banks, both initially and subsequent to the commencement of operations. ICOF assisted in five cases and one or other of the central government bodies provided initial funds for four groups and further funds for a total of five groups. Charities gave some funds to three groups.

Of the amount of finance required over half the operating co-operatives, and almost all of those planned, needed over £5,000. Only two of the operating groups required initial finance of less than £1,000.

Other Resources

There was surprising conformity among the groups as far as other resources were concerned. The vast majority used the skills which their members already possessed both for operation and management. The authors had expected that in many cases the workers would be unskilled and that training would be obtained from internal sources. This was seldom the case in either planned or operating groups. The decision as to the product to make, or service to provide, was in general based on either the skills of the group members or the identification of a sales opportunity, each being of roughly equal proportions in both operating and planned groups. A few groups had, however, been formed with the express purpose of providing a particular product or service.

Many of the groups received advice, when setting up, from ICOM itself and from common ownership companies. The latter were by far the most important in providing general advice. Only a few groups received advice from trade unions, teachers, community workers or banks, and over one-third of the operating groups received no outside help at all. Over one-half of the established groups and almost all of those planned had both business experience and some contact with other co-operatives. Strange to say, the more recently established groups had less initial contact with other co-operatives than the older groups.

Internal Organisation

The characteristics which should in practice distinguish co-operatives from conventional businesses are those which relate to the manner of decision-making, the arrangement of jobs, the determination of wages and the distribution of any surplus. According to the authors many of the groups which replied to the questionnaire would appear to the purist, to fail as co-operatives in one or more of these respects.

Over one-quarter of the operating groups do not indulge in communal decision-making and half of the planned groups do not intend to do so. Furthermore, in three groups, those responsible for making decisions are not elected by the rest of the workforce and are, presumably, therefore less rigidly accountable to them.

One-third of the operating groups do not have a policy of job rotation even in a restricted sense and in only half the cases are all jobs rotated. This situation is less pronounced in the case of the planned co-operative. It is appreciated of course that in a manufacturing concern it is not very easy to employ a job rotation policy.

With regard to wage levels, nearly one-third of the established co-operatives had no restrictions on pay differentials. Eleven, however, had a limit of less than 2:1 between the highest and lowest paid, i.e., very little differential at all. In the majority of the operating groups pay levels are determined arbitrarily, on the basis of what can be afforded in terms of current profits etc. or individual needs. None of the groups pay wages in accordance with union or market rates. In over half the groups, pay is not related to production, sales or hours worked. Only in three cases was seniority mentioned as being a factor in determining pay. Most co-operatives try to avoid the problems of piece work or commission systems. They were established with the particular intention of avoiding the evils of "capitalistic" organisations and in a manufacturing company piece work systems are considered as being "soul destroying" assembly line jobs.

Profits

In few cases (only four of the established groups) were there fixed rules for the distribution of any surplus. The majority of groups stated that the distribution could be arrived at by agreement at the time, and indeed a number replied that there was no surplus to distribute anyway. While the majority stated that any surplus would be distributed within the group, 40 per cent stated that at least a part would go outside. In these cases the recipients would usually be organisations having similar aims to these co-operatives, e.g., community groups.

Perceived Future Problems

With regard to future problems as perceived by the operating groups, eleven mentioned the maintenance of the co-operatives structure as being one of their worries. Other problems mentioned were the keeping of staff (6); profits, wage levels, job security (5); finance (2); and coping with fast growth (2).

Summary and Conclusions

The operating groups which responded to the questionnaire differ greatly in a number of respects. From the point of view of size, 14 had less than 10 workers, while two had 30 or more. The majority had sales of less than £40,000 per annum. Three groups had changed from private to common ownership and in these the emphasis is on co-operative ownership of the business and its rewards in terms of job satisfaction. Many of the more recently formed groups are described by the authors as being part of the "alternative society" most of them being wholefood shops or "radical" publishers. In these groups the interest is on co-operation in practice, on the day-to-day running of the groups, on the resolution of problems and on the determination of policy. Common to all groups, however, is the fact that they have structural problems to overcome in addition to the normal commercial difficulties. These problems are related to "people" mainly, and are brought about by the very fact of co-operative organisation. They might be likened to industrial relations problems in conventional firms, but according to the authors they are perhaps less easily solved than such problems. This is a rather sobering thought when it is considered that co-operatives are often thought of as being the answer to many of our industrial relations problems.

Most of the established groups appear to be financially secure and successful. Some of those more recently started appear less robust commercially, although the same would be true for many conventional companies begun only a few years back. Reasons for the establishment of co-operatives accorded with the authors' expectations. The longer established groups tend to be concerned with replacing the inequities implicit in conventional employment and seem often to have been founded on *Christian principles*. More of the newer groups combine an interest in their product with an interest in their internal organisation and manifest a preference for an *alternative society*. The planned groups, on the other hand, are being organised on behalf of, rather than by, those who will work in them (in contrast to the older groups), and have as their prime motivation the provision of employment.

The planned groups hope to rely predominantly on grant aid. This, together with the aim of providing employment, explains why the average number of workers planned is double that of the other groups. The planned groups are attempting to concentrate on labour intensive work but this raises the question as to whether they will succeed in building up to commercially viable rates of turnover within the time permitted by the provision of the grant. The experience of other groups may be relevant in this regard.

One group in the light industry trade which was formed with a trade union subscription for the retraining of disabled miners was forced at one stage to make them all redundant in order that those with skill could produce at a low enough cost to put the firm back on its feet. Another group, which was started by a charitable trade for the purpose of offering apprentice training in the building industry to unemployed young people was forced for the same reason to reduce the apprentice/tradesman ratio from 5:1 to 1:1. This fact goes to show that attempts to create industrial employment through labour intensive enterprises is a hazardous undertaking. Service enterprises, if they could be organised, would have a better chance of success.

Financial Survival

Chaplin and Cowe state that very many new co-operatives have been established specifically to avoid the economic pressures which are a central feature of the ordinary business world. Their members appear to behave in a very different manner from that which would be expected of the typical "economic man". The authors state, however, that these factors may be relevant in the short-term only and that in the long run co-operative workers will behave as most employees do. This certainly happened in the past; seemingly dedicated workers took too much in wages, did not plough back sufficient for the replacement and renewal of capital stock and as a result businesses went broke.

There are, of course, a number of reasons for the decline in the number of traditional producer co-operatives. Many have been in difficult industries (clothing and footwear) while others had characteristics which lead to a more rapid turnover of firms than usual (e.g., printing). Furthermore, the whole of the co-operative movement has had significant business problems which could well be due to its lack of attractiveness to managers, leading to considerable management shortcomings. Unfortunately, co-operatives are often too small to be able to afford a professional manager while the larger ones have difficulty in attracting good men because of wage differential policy.

The fact that British co-operatives must survive within a capitalistic economy has a bearing on the struggle to maintain co-operation in practice as well as in name—a struggle which was too great for the co-operative movement in the last century. But perhaps the times have changed sufficiently for the new co-operative movement to survive, learning to some extent from previous failures. Spokesmen for the movement point to some reason for optimism. When asked if the new co-operatives are the first of many, or are merely a brief flicker destined to be blown out they say:

> The problems are no greater than those overcome by earlier trade unions and co-operators. Moreover our predecessors lacked what we have now—the asset of political power to aid our efforts of industrial organisation. (Chaplin and Cowe, 1977, p. 52)

Chapter 4

*Spain – The Mondragon Movement**

The Mondragon movement in Spain is in many ways the most interesting example of workers' co-operatives in capitalistic countries. Mondragon is a small town in the Spanish Basque country about 30 miles from Bilbao, which has become the headquarters of a very large co-operative movement. Twenty-five years ago this district was a poor under-developed region. Today it is a thriving industrial centre. The co-operatives are spaced over four provinces and occupy an area little larger than the six counties of Northern Ireland with a total population of about 3.0 million. The active labour force numbers 1.05 million of which about 15 per cent are employed in agriculture, forestry and fishing, 48 per cent in industry and 37 per cent in the services. The unemployment rate is about 10-12 per cent.

The history of the Mondragon movement goes back to 1943 when a Basque priest (Father Arizmendi, a veteran of the Civil War on the Republican side) founded a technical college specialising in metallurgy. It was planned from the start to provide social as well as technical education and the students were taught that people in industry should work together for mutual and community benefit.

The original educational system was a two-year course aimed to provide training for young people so that they could

*This description is based on the following: Campbell *et al.*, 1977; Campbell and Foster, 1974; Johnson and Whyte, 1977 as well as from information gained by one of the authors (P. Kelly) who visited Mondragon in October 1978.

qualify as skilled workers upon entering employment. In succeeding years the college programme was expanded to include instruction up through college level leading to engineering degrees, while the student body was expanded from 24 in the first year to over 1,500 today. The school is not confined to co-operative workers' children. It is open to all. In 1956 five young men who had graduated from the college in 1952 formulated a plan to set up a worker-owned enterprise. Local support was forthcoming from other workers and in November of that year, 23 men started making paraffin cookers. By 1959 the membership of this co-operative, called Ulgor, had increased to 170; gas cookers were now being produced and six other off-shoot co-operatives had just been started. Three of the latter joined with a consumer co-operative in setting up a workers' bank (The Caja Laboral Popular). The workers were at first very sceptical of getting involved in banking but Fr Arizmendi argued that co-operatives could not develop to their full potential without capital, that credit would not be available to them under acceptable conditions through private banks and that therefore they must build their own banking system. This they did within two years after the founding of Ulgor.

Today the number of Mondragon industrial enterprises has increased to 58, with a total of 16,000 members, of which one-third are women. In addition there are a number of agricultural, service, educational and consumer co-operatives. There is equal pay for equal work but women tend to be employed in less responsible posts. The annual turnover is £300 million. The workers' bank has 76 branches, private deposits totalling £180 million and capital and reserves amounting to £14 million. Control of the bank is 50 : 50 between the operating enterprises and the bank staff. The bank acts as the co-ordinating centre of the group, providing sophisticated management services, assisting with short-and-long-term planning and monitoring the progress of its member co-operatives. In the early days the Caja also handled social security payments in the area. Under Spanish law the self-employed did not qualify for state social security and since the co-operatives are owned by the labour force, the workers are considered to be self-employed. Thus a separate social security system was required from the outset. From 1958 to 1974 this was handled by a separate division of the bank. In 1974 an independent second-degree co-operative, called Lagun-Aro, was established to handle social welfare. This organisation provides family allowances, medical insurance, sickness benefits, widow's and normal retirement pensions, etc. Its services are paid for by deductions from wages. To discourage malingering a member forgoes salary and receives no benefit for the first three days of an illness. There is thus an exceptionally low rate of absenteeism. Also medical fees (heavily subsidised) are paid directly for all medical services received. This helps to ensure that the Community's services are used responsibly. The principle applied is: "Each man should use what he needs, all that he needs and only what he really needs". (Campbell, *et al.*, 1977, p. 52.)

In the years following the formation of the first industrial firm, the educational system developed an additional supporting institution. This is called Alecoop, a co-operative factory which produces components for other firms in the complex and also takes on jobs in the open market. The interesting thing about this factory is, that the college students work in it for five hours a day to earn tuition and living expenses so that they can devote another five hours to their educational programme. Recently, also, the system set up a £1 million research and development institution designed to undertake projects of long-term importance that cannot be expected to yield short-run benefits to particular firms. Another supporting institution is the League for Education and Culture, a broad association of parents, teachers, students and supporters from the community. The League has played an important role in linking the educational system to the co-operative firms and to the community in general while it has helped to work out legal and political problems with municipalities and with the national government.

In brief then, the Mondragon industrial co-operative complex is built on three institutional bases, namely:

1. The educational system, including (a) the technical college, (b) the Alecoop to finance the students and (c) the research and development laboratories to undertake pilot schemes.
2. The League of Education and Culture to link the educational system to the firms and to the community in general, and
3. the bank or credit union which supports the whole organisation and is responsible for expansion of the co-operatives.

A diagramatic representation of how the system works is shown in Figure 1.

The Management Growth

The expansion of the co-operatives has been managed in two ways; through the fission of existing firms and through the creation of new firms by the workers' bank. The growth and fission of firms has been made possible by the reinvestment policy of the system. According to the original programme, which has been maintained with little variation, the surplus (profit) of the co-operatives is divided into three parts at the end of each financial year. A total of 30 per cent is set aside for two purposes; 10 to 15 per cent goes for social benefit to the community (including support of the educational system) and the remaining 15-20 per cent is set aside as a reserve fund to be maintained by the co-operative firms. The remaining 70 per cent is distributed to the members in proportion to the hours worked during the year and the rate of pay received. This is normally deposited to an account which each member holds with his firm. The account is treated by the firm as a

FIGURE 1: DIAGRAM OF THE MONDRAGON MOVEMENT

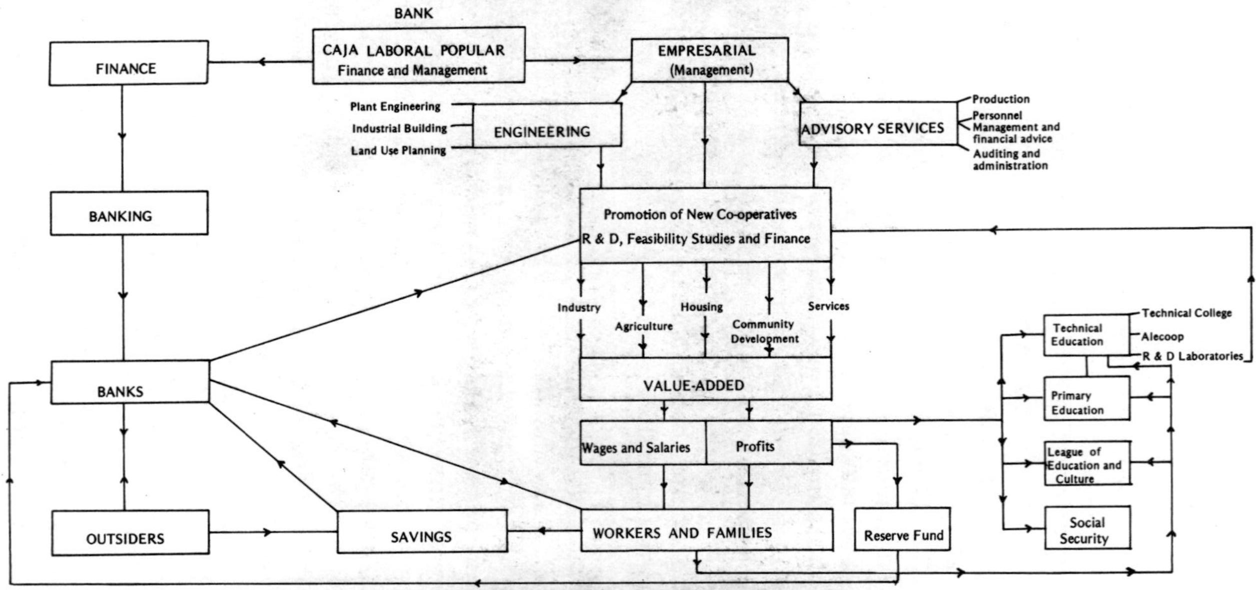

debt to the members on which interest is paid annually. The minimum interest paid is six per cent per annum but this is increased to take account of the cost of living and of profitability. In recent years members have been receiving about 13 per cent on their accounts.

A member in good standing, who leaves the firm with proper notice to join a capitalistic firm, is allowed to take out 80 per cent of the money deposited in his account; the firm keeps the balance. If a member is discharged for disciplinary reasons or leaves without notice, the firm may retain up to 30 per cent of his account. If a member moves to another co-operative within the system, after giving due notice, his account is automatically transferred to the new firm. When a member reaches retirement age he may withdraw 100 per cent of the money in his account. There have been few retirements so far but to avoid serious drains on capital in future years, the bank will try and persuade people to take annuities rather than lump sum payments. These payments will be additional to any contributory pensions paid by the Lagun-Aro.

Mondragon's principle of crediting 70 per cent of profits to workers' accounts is unusual. Most co-operatives adopt the principle of collective ownership so that the assets are owned by the entire workforce as a group which changes with time. No individual has the right to draw on and enjoy a personal share of the assets and he receives no pay-out when he leaves. There are arguments for and against each of these systems but there is no doubt that individual ownership has proved a strong motivating force in Mondragon.

Size of Organisation

The founders of the Mondragon system believed that it would be easier to maintain a true co-operative with small organisations than with large ones. Therefore as a firm reached a point where it developed a new line of production that could provide a basis for a new firm, that new firm was spun-off the original. Thus the original firm, Ulgor, has given rise to six other firms. The earnings of all these firms are, however, pooled and workers can shift from one to another within the group. This federation called Ularco has now over 6,000 members, of which Ulgor accounts for over 3,000. This is considered too large but so far attempts to break it down into smaller groups have failed.

In 1977 the other 50 or so co-operatives in Mondragon averaged a labour force of around 100, the size breakdown of the whole group, including Ularco, being as follows:

No. of workers	*No. of co-operatives*
0 – 100	26
100 – 250	14
250 – 500	11
500 – 1,000	6
1,000 +	1
Total	58

In 1977 the industrial spread of the group as a whole was:

Type of production	*Number of co-operatives*	*Number of workers*
Consumer durables and furniture	10	4,323
Machine tools	14	2,678
Intermediate goods and components and miscellaneous	23	3,736
Foundries and forges	6	1,309
Construction and building materials	5	1,237
Total	58	13,284

In addition to these there are two service co-operatives, one operated entirely by women who provide laundry and catering services to the factories. There are five agricultural and five housing co-operatives associated to the group. Apartment blocks are built by the housing co-operatives on behalf of co-operative workers, to whom the bank advances a substantial proportion of the initial costs. There is also one consumer co-operative which was established in 1969. In 1975 it had 30 branches distributed over the region and 50,000 consumer members. Surplus profits instead of being paid as a dividend to the consumers is allocated in the same way as it is in the producers' co-operatives.

Finally, there are six educational co-operatives, one social security co-operative, one research and development centre as well as the bank itself. The educational co-operatives consist of the original technical college (now a university) and five primary and technical schools, catering for 1,500 students. One of the attractions of these schools is that the Basque language is used for teaching; until recently this was forbidden in state schools since the Civil War. These second degree service co-operatives are of special significance in that they demonstrate how a community's social needs can be served in a co-operative system and thus how a strong co-operative sector can provide for the welfare of its community.

The Bank (Caja Laboral Popular)

Because the bank is such a vital institution in the running of the organisation its operation is described in some detail below. As stated above the bank was one of the earliest institutions established at Mondragon as the co-operatives needed a reliable source of finance to cover liquidity needs and expansion plans, and also an institution to handle social security for the group. The bank originally started in two small offices, one in the school and one in the headquarters of Catholic Action; the five founders of Ulgor devoted a good deal of their time to handle the paper work. In 1959 the bank achieved more formal status, being registered as a savings co-operative. Offices were opened simultaneously in two provinces in case either provincial administration should take action against the initiative.

The bank gradually developed its three main functions:

1. The provision of social security up to 1974 when the Lagun-Aro was founded.
2. The channelling of local savings to provide finance for the industrial co-operatives; and
3. the provision of management advice to the co-operatives.

The bank is allowed by law to pay interest to its members at a half per cent above the normal deposit rate and as a result the community was quick to place its savings in the bank for the creation of new jobs. In the eight years between 1966 and 1974 the number of savers and the amount of savings multiplied enormously. Despite this increase, the expansion of the co-operatives was restricted by the availability of finance from the bank, up to 1972. Since then deposits have exceeded requirements.

Because the bank's investments are spread among a small number of clients (77 active member co-operatives) the risks from concentration are high. To counter-balance this, the bank has, from the start, had to provide a very strong management back-up for its members; this high degree of control and monitoring has resulted so far in few failures and bad debts.

The first line of defence lies in the contract of association between the bank and an individual co-operative; this lays down the ground rules for management in considerable detail. Secondly, before a co-operative is established, the bank undertakes a very detailed feasability study, which normally takes one to two years. Thirdly, the bank monitors the operation of all existing co-operatives; they are required to supply monthly operating statistics which are regularly checked against annual and five-year plans. The division of the bank, which deals with management (The Empresarial Division) currently has a staff of 90 people.

Ultimate control of the bank rests with the General Assembly of members. This comprises the staff of the bank, plus representatives of member co-operatives. For industrial co-operatives there is one member per 20 employees, one representative per 200 members of consumer and agricultural co-operatives and one representative per co-operative for educational and housing co-operatives. Up to 1975 savers were also members with one representative per 1,000 at the General Assembly; this has now been forbidden by Spanish Law and so has had to be discontinued. The General Assembly elects a Control Board which in turn appoints the Executive Management. The main decisions of the bank are taken by a Management Council which meets once a month. This Council includes the Director and Assistant Director of the bank, the heads of the different banking divisions and a legal adviser.

The total staff of the bank is 467, of which 123 are employed at head office and 344 in the 64 local branch offices. The contract of association between co-operatives and the bank is a lengthy document which governs the basic legal relationship between the bank and each co-operative. In summary form it states that:

1. The co-operative will become a member of the bank's General Assembly and will abide by its decision.
2. The co-operative will provide a legal guarantee of the bank's capital and will contribute to its social fund.
3. It will provide the bank with an annual profit and loss account, a plan for the forthcoming year and monthly operating data.
4. Surplus liquidity will be deposited in the bank for lending to other co-operatives.
5. The co-operative must adhere to the basic policies of the group, i.e., democratic control, fund interest on workers' capital, contribute to community funds, and extend membership to all employees.

6. The co-operative will adhere to the basic economic rules of the group which specify that not less than 30 per cent of surplus profits shall be divided between a reserve fund and a social fund; all members shall contribute a capital stake (payable over not more than two years) and shall receive interest of not less than six per cent on this capital.
7. Salaries shall vary by not more than a ratio of 3:1, but executives may be paid up to 50 per cent over their basic salary to take account of unpaid overtime, special responsibilities, etc. Salary levels shall be established by comparison with local industries.

Almost from the beginning, but especially in the last few years, the bank has been remarkably profitable, so much so that it would be unfair if its staff should share in enterprise profits in the same way as do the worker members of the industrial co-operatives. The bank's staff thus receive as its profits share, a sum equal to the average distributed in the group as a whole. It is an arrangement which obviously strengthens the feeling of solidarity between the bank and the directly productive enterprises.

Services Provided by the Bank

The managerial (Empresarial) division of the bank is perhaps the most important feature of the whole undertaking. Experience elsewhere has shown that management weaknesses are the major problem of producer co-operatives. Indeed management carried out by the workers has often been irresponsible and short-sighted. To overcome this difficulty it is the responsibility of the bank to guide the launching of new co-operatives and to monitor and advise established enterprises. The management charges the individual enterprises for its standard services but no attempt is made to make the unit 100 per cent self-financing.

The planning and launching of a new co-operative is a highly structured process. In the early days, groups of potential co-operators would approach the bank with their schemes carefully planned, at least to the type of product and basic organisation. Recently the bank has encouraged groups of workers to approach them if they would like to build a new co-operative, even if they have no clear idea about what to produce or how to do the job. The one overriding consideration, according to the bank, is that the first initiative should come from the workers, this means that the nucleus of the labour force is committed from the start to trying to make a co-operative venture work. The group is also expected to select a manager, but if no suitable talent is available within the group, the bank will put up three or four candidates from whom one can be chosen.

The manager, once selected, is seconded to the management section of the bank for up to two years. His salary is paid by the bank, but this is treated as a debt incurred by the future co-operative. One member of the management section becomes the "godfather" of the co-operative and he and the selected manager work closely together on the preparation of plans for the new enterprise. Once a product has been chosen, the market prospects are studied closely over a five-year perspective, methods of production are studied and the two will probably visit a number of the more advanced firms in the field, either in Spain or abroad. The necessary capital investment will also be assessed as well as methods of financing. It is found in practice that each "godfather" can handle two or three incipient co-operatives simultaneously. The bank can thus launch four or five new co-operatives a year.

Finance is an important consideration in planning a new enterprise. The co-operators are expected to put up roughly 20 per cent of starting capital; a further 20 per cent is available from a government co-operative loan fund at three per cent interest, the remainder is put up by the bank. Shortage of finance often rules out the most capital intensive methods of manufacture.

How Failures are Dealt With

Campbell, *et al.* (1977, p.45) report some interesting examples of Mondragon co-operatives which failed. They say that in the late 1960s the government offered fishermen large grants in order to buy their own boats and run them as co-operatives. It was for this reason that the fishermen approached the Mondragon Caja (bank) for loans to cover the residual capital required. In the event, the state contributed 71 per cent of the capital requirement, the Caja and other sources 24 per cent and the fishermen themselves five per cent. The initiative did not prove profitable and it was wound up by the state. The failure is explained on two grounds: the very low level of understanding of co-operative philosophy among the fishermen and their low level of capital involvement. One might also draw the conclusion that a co-operative system imposed by the state, rather than arising from the workers' own initiative has much reduced chances of success.

Another co-operative began by manufacturing machine tools under licence for a British firm, but the line did not prove economically viable. The place almost closed down for a few months with most of the workers being sent home on full pay or given temporary jobs. The remaining workers, however, ripped out the machinery and moved on to an entirely new production line, which now profitably employs all the original workers. The Caja provided the bridging finance and was the architect of the change over.

A problem which has not been solved is the conversion of the local hospital into a co-operative. As the hospital is used extensively by Lagun-Aro patients, it appeared logical to have the hospital convert itself into a full member of the co-operative community. The barrier lay in persuading the doctors to accept the standard 3:1 salary differential. It appears from this that highly trained members of the professional classes are less prepared to make financial sacrifices than the management class.

Finally, there is the story of Mondragon's one and only

strike. This erupted in Ulgor in 1974 and lasted about a week. A work study team had been brought in to reassess salary differentials. As a result some jobs were up-graded and some down-graded within the 3:1 point system. The management had agreed beforehand that there would be no reductions in salary; jobs would only revert to their lower point grading when a worker was replaced. Nevertheless the insult to down-graded workers' pride led to the eruption. The management board decided that 17 leaders of the strike should be sacked and 297 others receive lesser penalties. Although the strike leaders challenged this decision at a meeting of the full membership of the co-operative, the decision was upheld.

This was a very painful experience as far as the "thinkers" of the movement were concerned. It demonstrated the near impossibility of establishing adequate channels of communication within a very large co-operative (Ulgor has over 3,000 members). It also turned their attention to the experiments being made in Sweden and Norway (notably at Volvo) in adapting production processes to take account of the workers involved, particularly in scrapping production lines and replacing them with start-to-finish assembly by a small group.

Restructuring of organisation on the Scandinavian model has been experimented with at Ulgor and at other organisations including the bank itself. These innovations, where adopted, have improved efficiency, but Ulgor has been held back in re-organisation by the economic problems of dismantling costly production lines and by the unwillingness of most production workers to change from familiar methods. The "thinkers" have therefore concluded that Ulgor must be left to muddle through with its large staff and old production line organisation. As new co-operatives are set up, however, two considerations will in future be introduced at the initial planning stage.

1. The maximum size to which a co-operative should be allowed to grow is around 400-500 employees, and

2. production methods should be designed to use the mind as well as the hands of the worker and to allow flexibility in scheduling—a small group should be able to take a day off when they wish and make up by extra hours on other days.

Discussion

The remarkable record of commercial success of the Mondragon co-operatives in the recent past indicates that they have found a workable solution to the application of co-operative principles in modern industry. The question, however, remains as to whether their solution is only workable in the Basque country or could it be imitated elsewhere, particularly in Ireland and Britain.

One must ask is the Mondragon success primarily the result of the organisational structure which has evolved or is it due to special geographic and historic factors? Both have clearly played a part. Historically, we must bear in mind that the Basques, who have strong separatist ambitions, had supported the losing Republican side in the Spanish Civil War and this left them in the post-war years with their economy in ruins and a central government which was highly suspicious of the political overtones of any Basque initiative.

In its contradictory way this probably provided the perfect breeding ground for the co-operative movement. In the first place there was an unemployed labour force hungry for work. Secondly, since the whole economy had to be rebuilt there were many industrial opportunities. Spain's post-war isolationist policy made these opportunities easy to grasp by warding off overseas competition; and most importantly, Basque nationalism, denied a political outlet, ensured strong community backing for this strictly regional initiative. In it, according to Campbell, *et al.* (1977) the local people saw a means of rebuilding their world. Though Mondragon is located only 30 miles from Bilbao and there is a motorway for part of the way, the journey takes an hour by car on account of the mountains. Also there is no rail link. Their isolated situation plus the presence of four large steel producing firms within a radius of 10 miles provided a promising environment for industrial initiatives.

One further point should be mentioned. Trade unions have been illegal in Spain throughout the period of Mondragon's evolution. The ban was lifted in 1977 and Mondragon's "thinkers" are already wondering how this is likely to affect their group. On the one hand, they would wish their members to join unions in order to maintain working class solidarity. On the other hand, they have no wish to see their worker-owned enterprises undermined by irrelevant sympathy strikes, or their sensitively structured organisation of industrial relations upset.

The question of the extent to which replicable and non-replicable factors have been involved in the Mondragon success can also be approached from a consideration of its ideology. Historically this seems to have started as a combination of progressive Catholic social doctrines and traditional working class aspirations, on the one hand, and a strong commitment to the "primacy of work", on the other. But though the motivation of the surviving founding members, derives partly from these sources, it is clear that a progressive Basque nationalism is now the most important driving force. It is plausible, of course, to argue that constructive forces other than nationalism might be mobilised elsewhere to supply the necessary drive. An exceptionally high level of unemployment in Ireland with few emigration outlets could act to stimulate interest in co-operatives and get projects started.

Chapter 5

*Israel**

The process of building an independent labour managed economy in Israel was conceived through various channels, long before the establishment of the present state. In the early years of this century groups of young immigrants to Palestine strove to express their beliefs and expectations in various ways, but all were in agreement around one general objective, the creation of a new Jewish workers' society in the ancient "Homeland". Though differing in their views about the shape which the new ideal society should take, they were united in the fundamental belief that the labour movement must assume central responsibility for developing and building up the country, and preparing conditions for the economic, social, and cultural absorption of the masses of new immigrants returning at the time.

Separate groups, however, jealously maintained their own sets of values; the debate stormed between those who believed in the collective (Kibbutz) and those who strove to live in co-operatives of individuals (Moshav Ovdim); between the large open Kibbutz and the more intimate (enclosed) "Kvutza". Others argued in favour of consumer co-operatives and discussed whether they should encompass the entire population or serve only their own closed ring of members. Others still concentrated on the problems which were likely to besiege the other part of the independent labour economy, the so

*The material on Israel presented here is taken mainly from Adizes, Ichak and Elizabeth Mann Borgese, 1975; Jenkins, David, 1973; Stettner, Leonora, 1977; Daniel, Abraham, 1976; and Klatzmann, Joseph, 1963.

called administrative sector—how to combine the whole movement towards some of the major objectives of national and social importance. This sector was developed by the Histadrut (General Federation of Labour in Israel) which assembled people and some capital on a voluntary basis and built up a technologically advanced economy on a magnitude experienced in few countries.

We give below a brief account of each of these main sections of the labour economy in Israel.

The Kibbutzim

The Kibbutzim of Israel are in many ways the most remarkable co-operatives in the world. According to Jenkins (1973, p. 73) they have lasted longer than any similar type of organisation in the world, are still thriving today and have survived wars, economic turbulence and their own mini-industrial revolution.

The Kibbutzim are, however, more than a group of ordinary co-operatives. They are a political focal point as well, and were heavily involved in building the nation of Israel. But they are more than just frontier settlements. Bristling with cultural, ideological and educational activities they have also developed the most modern agricultural system in the world. In 1975 there were 94,000 people living in 230 Kibbutzim.

There are six separate Kibbutz movements which were founded at different times and trace their origins to different parts of Europe. There are important differences in ideology between these movements; one, for example, embraces the strict religious adherents, while another is an integral part of the Labour Party. Each of the movements has a central organisation for such matters as mutual aid, purchasing, marketing, training and education, and the development of new settlements. Five of the six movements came together in 1963 to form a federation which organises a wide range of co-operative activities. Nevertheless, there is still a great deal of variety among them, depending on location and type of economic activity: as well as the conjuncture of personalities (Kennedy, 1976).

All Kibbutzim are thoroughly democratic and have been from the beginning. Every major discussion is approved by a general meeting in which each member has a vote. Members are given jobs, as far as possible, according to their own wishes and capabilities. Members are rotated between jobs, including supervisory posts. Nobody receives any real "salary" and everyone receives equal treatment regarding his basic needs—housing, food, clothing and a minimal allotment of pocket money. Private property is, strictly speaking a violation of the Kibbutz principles and for many years even such simple personal possessions as radios and tea-making equipment were frowned upon. Children are raised in common and all decisions regarding their education are made by the collective.

In the first decades of Kibbutz history the principles held up well. Hard physical labour, austerity and devotion to ideals of brotherhood and equality provided a winning combination. Since nobody was ever forced to remain on a Kibbutz if he did not want to stay, the mere fact that they survived and even steadily grew in number is adequate evidence that the principles worked well. Whatever the difficulties, the ideology and the abundant other satisfactions were adequate to maintain the Kibbutzim as living institutions.

But as in all things, change must come and change came to the Kibbutzim in the form of their own little industrial revolution. During the Second World War the British army, as well as the Kibbutzim themselves, needed various processed food items and manufactured products. To provide these a number of the Kibbutzim established industrial production facilities alongside the agricultural operations. At first this was a temporary measure, but as time passed industrialisation made further gains for different reasons. Advances in agricultural productivity rapidly reduced the need for workers, and since the amount of additional land available was limited, there was no room to re-employ redundant workers in further agricultural production.

Under Kibbutz ideology, however, jobs had to be created for surplus workers and this was done through industrialisation. At first the development was greeted with a good deal of scepticism by Kibbutz members but the practical forces were compelling. "The realities were stronger than the principles" (Jenkins, p. 77). At present about two-thirds of the Kibbutzim have industrial operations employing a total of about 11,000 persons. Many have several factories each, and in a few cases two or more Kibbutzim have combined to form relatively large industrial units. The Kibbutzim industries include canning, metalwork, plastics, furniture, chemicals and building materials. Growth in industrial production is outpacing that in agriculture and more plants are steadily being added.

Unfortunately industrialisation has brought in its wake a less welcome development–the hiring of outside workers on a regular wage basis. This came about because there were not sufficient Kibbutz members available to staff the factories to the required level. It was thought at first that the taking on of hired workers would be temporary, but as things turned out this was not so. It has continued because of a continued shortage of Kibbutz members and because of the need for highly trained persons. Today almost all the Kibbutz industrial operations have outside workers, some only a small number, others several hundred. The largest Kibbutz factory is a plywood operation at Afikim, employing 320 outside workers and only 40 Kibbutz members. On average, the number of hired workers is about 60 per cent of the total. The trend is seen as a disruption of Kibbutz principles because the outside workers have shown no inclination to become members. A few small factories have succeeded in getting rid of the hired workers and replacing them by members, but generally economies of scale require a large labour force, most of whom must be hired.

Though the Kibbutzim have been notably successful in

both their agricultural and industrial enterprises, writers who have studied the movement are pessimistic about creating Kibbutzim outside Israel and, indeed, as will be shown later, efforts to transfer the Kibbutz spirit to ordinary industry within Israel have not been very successful either. The movement is too collective for all but a small number of people.

The Kibbutz movement lives and develops in its own fashion. It withstands stresses that are created from the proximity of an environment with an entirely different point of view and way of life. It finds new members from all over the world, but at the same time there is a falling away of young people, many of whom are attracted to urban life. About 15-20 per cent of those born in the Kibbutzim leave for the outside world at the end of their school days. The movement, however, continues to play a significant part in the social and communal life of the country and its influence can be judged from the members among Government Ministers, Histadrut members and Labour Party leaders. Hence despite the changes which have taken place, the ideological front on which the movement stands is still a dominant force in the structure of the society of Israel.

The Moshav Ovdim

These differ from the Kibbutzim in that they are based on small holdings cultivated independently by each family, but within the context of the services supplied by the co-operative villages. These co-operative services include the purchase of inputs and of a large part of the consumer requirements of members, sale of produce, joint financing and credit, water supply, tractor stations, incubators, professional counselling services, educational, health, and cultural services, and mutual aid to members in need. New families are allocated plots of land leased from the state which are equal in size and quality and cannot be divided, increased or rented. Inheritance is decided by the family or failing that by the village. Families live in separate homes.

This form of co-operative has proved more acceptable to the recent immigrants and hence the Moshav Ovdim have been growing in numbers faster than the Kibbutzim. They now embrace 135,000 people in 378 villages, and account for 81 per cent of eggs marketed in Israel, 60 per cent of poultry, 50 per cent of milk as well as 34 per cent of fruit plantations. On the other hand, they are constantly having to cope with the problem of the uneconomic size of the farms and the unwillingness of young people to stay on the farms with the consequent need to undertake industrial projects.

These difficulties have led to efforts to combine the economies of scale of the Kibbutzim, on the one hand, with the household privacy of the Moshavim, on the other, in a new institutional form known as Moshav Shitafi. This is similar to a Kibbutz in that land is held and cultivated as a single unit. Equality of consumption is assured through the payment, not of wages, but of monthly allowances based on family composition. On the other hand, each family lives privately in a house allocated to it for permanent use and the women spend only a few hours a day on collective work. To date only 22 of the latter type villages have been developed.

Distributive and Consumer Co-operatives

In addition to the Kibbutzim and Moshavim there are various types of marketing and distributive co-operatives in Israel as well as consumer and contracting societies. The consumer movement, in particular, is very large and widely distributed. As in Ireland these societies are not workers' co-operatives. The employees are practically all hired workers.

Producer Co-operatives (Non-Agricultural)

The first producer co-operatives in Israel were founded at the time the first Kibbutzim were established. According to Daniel (1976) two co-operatives of seamstresses were established in Jaffa and Jerusalem in 1909 while a group of teamsters and a small association of tailors were organised in

Jaffa around the same time. Two of the worker parties at that time, Poalei Zion and Hapoel Hatzair, were instrumental in the organisation of these co-operatives. Their framework was extremely weak, however, as a result of the limited resources at their disposal.

A change in the development of producer co-operatives took place in 1910 with the establishment of a co-operative print shop in Jerusalem. This enterprise was founded by Poalei Zion for the specific needs of its newsletter, Haechdut. From the beginning this enterprise ran into considerable trouble, but in the third year of its operation, it received assistance from The Palestine Workers' Fund, which saw the organisation and development of producer and service co-operatives, as one of its most important tasks.

When the First World War began, the activity of the Palestine Workers' Fund ceased and it was not renewed until 1919. With the Fund's help the Heachdut Press was then moved from Jerusalem to Jaffa. At the same time the Fund also assisted in the establishment of Carmel, a co-operative association of carpenters in Haifa; Amal a co-operative of metal workers in the same city; a carpenters co-operative in Jaffa and several other associations. However, despite the considerable assistance extended to them by the Fund, most of these co-operatives were dissolved in a relatively short period. It is claimed that the main reason for their dissolution lay in the fact that they were totally dependent on the Fund. The investment, all of which was made by the Fund, resulted in the loss of interest on the part of the members who considered themselves to some degree hired employees.

Additional evidence on the situation of producer and service co-operatives in Palestine during the first 30 years or so of this century is to be found in a study by Zvi Vitales published in July 1929 in the Newsletter, Commerce and Industry (quoted in Daniel, 1976, p. 206). In the Section devoted to producer co-operatives he wrote:

Although co-operative development in Palestine had not

> yet emerged from the period of its infancy, it had already served as a laboratory for many experiments in the branches of co-operative industrial production. Many of these experiments failed; others became partnerships or closed co-operatives. In 1926 there were 78 industrial producer co-operatives with 852 permanent workers; of these 663 were members of the co-operatives, 140 were hired workers and 49 were apprentices . . . Two years later, in December 1928, their number had decreased to 52 co-operatives with 663 permanent workers including 326 members and 337 hired employees. Forty-two of these co-operatives had less than seven members each and most of them employed less than five people. Three of eight co-operatives registered according to the Co-operative Societies Ordinance had less than the ten members required by law, so each of them was compelled to list Hevrat Ovdim Ltd (the industrial arm of the Histadrut) as more than one member.

This created serious problems for the co-operatives in question (*ibid.* p. 206). According to their statutes Hevrat Ovdim had a number of votes equal to the number of all other members of the association and it also held the right to veto decisions by the management committees and the general meetings. This condition was intended to protect the co-operative character of the enterprise, and not to intervene in the internal affairs of management, but in practice it did not always operate in this way. It proved restrictive and the co-operatives were often forced to take on extra hired workers, which they did not need.

The problems facing producer co-operatives around this time were spelled out in a report made for the Histadrut in 1926 which stated (*ibid.* p. 214) that these co-operatives were confronted by many complicated problems without the possibility of learning from previous experience of other societies. Each co-operative started upon its way anew and repeated the mistakes that the others had already overcome.

There was no permanent arrangement for the ownership of co-operative property. Shares or equal holdings were not customary in most of the co-operatives; one of the members might have invested more money in the business than others and wages were determined in strange ways. There were cases where profits were not divided equally among all the members.

With regard to finance, the credit of these co-operatives did not even amount to half of their monthly production, in spite of the fact that most of them had to keep stocks or finished goods equivalent to at least the value of one month's production. Since most of them did not have their own capital to finance current operations, they were compelled to make ends meet by a variety of stratagems beginning with expensive credit from their suppliers and ending in negotiable promissory notes: at the time all the co-operatives purchased their raw materials from local dealers. This financial strangulation compelled the managers of the co-operatives to occupy themselves almost entirely with the negotiation of promissory notes and the search for funds. Because of this they were forced to neglect all efforts for the improvement of their products, the reduction of their production costs and the improvement in productivity. In addition, most of the co-operatives lacked permanent legal status and because of this they had no possibility of appearing as clients of local banks. The only exception was the bank Hapoalim (the workers' bank) the one institution which helped the co-operatives as much as it could.

Following this report the First Congress of the Histadrut in July 1927 resolved to establish "A Co-operative Centre for Workshops, Manufacture and Public Services" as a central institution for the affairs of producer co-operatives. The functions of this institution were to include

1. Thorough and constant efforts for the development of workshops and factories on co-operative foundations,

2. the constant supervision and guidance of co-operatives and
3. the treatment of all economic, social and organisational problems of co-operatives.

For the development and consolidation of co-operative activity the Congress saw an urgent need for the creation of a special fund in the Bank Hapoalim to be devoted to the needs of producer co-operatives. It was considered necessary also that Hamashbir, a large co-operative wholesaling society, (which at that time included selling and buying operations) pay special attention to the sale of co-operative products and the purchase of raw material for them.

These were the primary functions with which the new centre was charged after its formation in January 1928 and its efforts were immediately aimed at restoring the producer co-operatives to economic health. Its first achievement was the formulation of model statutes which still serve today with only minor changes as the internal institutional basis for the producer and service co-operatives in Israel. It also organised campaigns for the improvement of work and production methods but despite these efforts the number of co-operatives declined to 42 by the end of 1929.

From 1928 to 1972, a period of 44 years—no essential change has taken place in the fundamental problems of producer and service co-operatives. The same problems that engaged the co-operative centre from its inception return periodically: financing, the relationship between Hevrat Ovdim and the co-operatives, and the need to improve efficiency and organisational problems such as pay shares and hired labour. Over the years there has never been much time for consolidation. National Zionist tasks such as immigration absorption, in-gathering of exiles and defence were always the dominant issues and tended to overshadow all other problems. Thus from the very beginning the Producer Co-operative Movement in Palestine was condemned to spontaneous intermittent development, feeling its way, as it were, through a continuous process of adaption to changing circumstances but never fully catching up.

In recent years, efforts on the part of co-operatives to catch up with technological developments in the economy have become apparent. Because the Co-operative Fund in the Bank Hapoalim has been operated very restrictively, producer and service co-operatives have been forced to go elsewhere for funds. Indeed a few have succeeded in raising the sum of I£5 million* from commercial financial institutions during 1970 partly on their own initiative and partly with the recommendation and help of the co-operative centre. These co-operatives also drew more than I£2 million from Hevrat Ovdim in the same year for consolidation and development.

In the metal and electrical industry, the co-operatives renewed their technological equipment, expanded industrial buildings and modernised their production methods. Co-operatives in the wood products' industry began to manufacture furniture for schools, hospitals and offices. Printing co-operatives developed special departments for offset and acquired modern equipment. Co-operatives in the construction materials' industry increased their output considerably by the introduction of modern equipment and scientific work methods.

On the other hand, 1970 brought no outstanding developments in other branches of producer co-operatives. Noteworthy among these are 30 co-operative bakeries that supply some 20 per cent of the country's demand for standard bread. Unification of these small co-operatives seems necessary if they are to survive in face of vigorous competition from capitalistic giants but so far they seem reluctant to do this.

In 1976 there were 73 producer co-operatives with 2,840 workers and an annual income of I£430 million (54 million

*£1 = Israeli Pound

US dollars). Largest of these was the Haargaz Co-operative which owns wood and metal working enterprises and accounts for 30 per cent of producer co-operative employees and income. It employs about 1,000 people, has an annual income of I£130 million, exports buses and various other products and provides packing crates for agricultural exports to the tune of about I£22 million. A high proportion of the employees are, however, hired workers.

Transport and Haulage Co-operatives

The beginning of motorised transport in Palestine dates from 1919. At this time the British Army began to sell surplus First World War vehicles to civilians and these soon began to be used for regular transportation service. During the 1920s groups of drivers began to organise co-operatives and in 1925 several organised groups operated in the Tel Aviv area. The large number of separate groups unavoidably resulted in disputes on the questions of route infringements, price competition and variations in wage rates. The Histadrut pressed for the restraint of competition and this along with severe public criticism of disputes resulted in a number of amalgamations into larger co-operatives. These mergers continued over the years so that when the state won independence in 1948 the transport of the country was carried on by five large co-operatives. Further mergers took place in subsequent years and by 1968, 98 per cent of all activity in public transportation was in the hands of two co-operatives Egged and Dan. Egged was responsible for inter-urban transport while urban transport was undertaken by Dan.

In 1976 total numbers employed in the two co-operatives were 11,000 of which about half were hired workers. Of the total labour force, Egged had 8,000 and Dan, 3,000. Total income of both co-operatives was about I£1,150 million (144 million US dollars). This is a large income for such an enterprise by international standards. At the beginning of 1977 these two co-operatives decided to unite to become possibly the largest co-operative transport enterprise in the world (Losh, 1979).

In addition to these two large transport enterprises, there are 19 road haulage co-operatives employing 1,500 workers and carrying 50 per cent of all haulage in Israel. The need for these to merge into larger organisations has not been so great and they appear to be doing their job adequately in competition with private firms.

Even though public transport is carried on by co-operatives, this branch of the economy in Israel has more or less the same problems as public transport in most countries. The great degree of concentration has planning and organisational advantages that serve the public interest, but on the other hand, because they are monopolies, the co-operatives are subject to strong governmental regulation with regard to fares and other matters: such regulation has very complex side-effects. One such effect seems to be that the financial position of the co-operatives has deteriorated greatly in recent years. According to Daniel (1976, p. 249) the accumulated deficit of Egged was I£95 million in 1970 while that of Dan was around I£70 million in the same year.

The immediate losses are met by loans and subsidies from the government but such funds do little to alleviate the causes of the trouble: if anything they partly account for them. A Commission appointed by the Ministry of Transport in 1966/67 to examine the situation of the transport co-operatives found that the increased deficits were due mainly to the wage rises granted to members over recent years. Had the wage increases for members been equal to those of the hired drivers, or to the average in the economy there would have been no deficit. The co-operatives might claim that fares were not allowed to rise sufficiently high but this is not so. In the five-year period from 1961/62 to 1965/66 fares in the two co-operatives rose by 90 per cent compared with an increase in the consumer price index of only 42 per cent.

The message from all this is obvious. A co-operative when given monopolistic powers acts in exactly the same way as an ordinary company and when the government stands by to take up the tab the co-operative has probably even fewer scruples than the company.

The Histadrut

The General Federation of Labour (Histadrut) which was founded in 1920, differs markedly from most other labour federations in the world. Though not a co-operative, its functions are so widespread and its influence so enormous that it has to be described in any discussion of Israeli Co-operatives.

The Histadrut embraces all the normal trade union activities, as well as operating residential workers colleges, institutes for higher education, a university college of labour studies, 60 trade schools and a vocational training course, study circles, youth clubs and a wide range of sports facilities. In addition it provides a number of social security institutions including provident funds, insurance (pension) funds for entire sectors of the economy, accident and dismissal compensation, loans to needy members, old age homes and childrens' institutions. Even more striking is the vast network of economic enterprise in agriculture, manufacturing, commerce and services for which the Histadrut is responsible through its economic arm, the Hevrat Ovdim.

Membership of the Histadrut is open to all men and women of the age of 18 and over earning their livelihood by their own labour. A worker joins the Histadrut directly, and through it becomes a member of one of some forty national unions according to his or her occupation. Members' wives may also be full members and young workers between the ages of 15 and 17 may belong to the Histadrut's Working Youth organisation.

The Histadrut, therefore, unites in a single organisation skilled and unskilled workers, members of co-operatives, other self-employed persons, housewives and working youths. In 1975 its adult membership comprised 1,286,600 workers while the working and student youth organisation had some 100,000 members. In addition some 166,660 workers and 36,600 housewives connected with smaller labour oragnisations outside the Histadrut have joined its trade unions and sick fund. Thus some 2,360,000 or 65 per cent of Israel's total population take part in, and benefit from, the Histadrut's activities.

Hevrat Ovdim

This is the economic arm of Histadrut and as such it comprises the same members and the same governing bodies. Although Hevrat Ovdim was originally conceived as a co-operative workers' society for settlement, industry, contracting and supply, its co-operative character has been somewhat diluted over the years. It now covers two basic types of organisation.

(a) Co-operatives run by their own members more or less autonomously, although they allocate some 10 per cent of their profits to Hevrat Ovdim and
(b) "institutional" enterprises collectively controlled by Hevrat Ovdim on behalf of the working community.

The co-operatives include the Kibbutzim, Moshavim, Distributive, Consumer, Producer and Service co-operatives.

The institutional enterprises are:

1. *Koor*: which is the largest concern in Israel, accounting for about one tenth of the country's industrial output. It produces metals, cement, glass, ceramics, plastics and chemicals and operates a large number of craft enterprises.
2. *Solel Boneh*: This is a building and Public Works Company which is responsible for more than 25 per cent of all building in Israel. It also has an overseas division which has undertaken intensive projects in a number of African, Mediterranean and Asian countries.
3. *Shikun Ovdim*: About one-third of Histadrut members,

or some 400,000 people live in workers' housing projects built by this organisation. Most of these are fully equipped apartments forming entire suburbs which are often organised as co-operative housing societies.

4. *Te'uss*: This is a special company organised jointly with the government to sponsor industrial undertakings in new development areas.
5. *Bank Hapoalim*: This is the major financial institution of the working class with 210 branches in 1973. It is the second largest bank in Israel.
6. *Hassneh* which is the largest insurance firm in Israel and operates in close co-operation with Bank Hapoalim.

In 1970 the institutional enterprises controlled by Hevrat Ovdim employed 240,000 people out of a national labour force of about one million. These enterprises are all managed by paid managers who are responsible to the Histadrut and not to the workers. The latter, who are also paid employees, differ in one important respect from workers in the other sectors of the economy. Their wages are not determined through negotiation procedures in the traditional way. They are decided unilaterally by the Histadrut and this decision binds all managements and workers.

The dual role of the Histadrut in being both an employer and a trade union is an unenviable one and has given rise to tensions and problems over the years. To diffuse these tensions wage scales and fringe benefits in the Histadrut enterprises are kept higher than in any other parts of the economy but this has not succeeded in solving the problem entirely. Bad relations between management and workers are a recurring feature of the sector.

In an effort to overcome the industrial relations difficulties and to restore some of the kibbutz spirit, the Histadrut at its eighth National Conference in 1958 passed a resolution on the participation of workers in the management of Histadrut projects. Little was done about it. However, at its tenth

National Conference in January 1966, the Histadrut adopted a stronger resolution "to arrange within a fixed period for the workers to participate in the management of the Histadrut enterprises, as well as to share in their profits and in the responsibility for achieving them". Those in favour of the resolution were confident that ordinary workers could make a valuable contribution to management and would become less militant as a result of this experience. As a first step in establishing worker participation, management/labour Councils were set up on an experimental basis in about a dozen Histadrut companies. The matters they were to deal with were firmly established in directives issued by the union's headquarters in Tel Aviv. This was the first mistake. One of the great strengths of the Kibbutzim is their flexible and informal character and the Histadrut effort at promoting democracy through the handing down of rigid statutes from above was out of tune with this movement. The result generally was that no actual progress was made. There was a lot of argument originally—the workers thought they were going to run the plants, but this never came about and after a while the workers themselves became discouraged. On the whole, therefore, the Histadrut plan for participation has shown few results. Writing in 1970 Jay Tabb, Professor of Industrial Relations at Haifa Technical University, said —

> In spite of 12 years of intentions, declarations and decisions . . . workers participation in management has still not been introduced in all Histadrut undertakings and in the few undertakings where joint managements have been established, it is doubtful whether they will last and succeed. (Quoted in Jenkins, 1973, p. 89)

The biggest problem up to that time seemed to be the resistance of managers to democracy.

Since 1970, however, some progress has been made. According to Adizes and Borgese (1975, p. 95) "Koor" the largest industrial concern in the Histadrut has introduced a method of participation in profits. In recent years the workers in fifteen plants have received considerable amounts of money as their share in profits and this has had a favourable influence on the feelings in the plants. However, the above writers state that profit sharing alone will not advance workers participation as a major development, unless it is linked with the decision-making process. Workers participation in the latter process has so far not been introduced on any widespread scale and it is doubtful if it will. There is a strong feeling in many quarters that management is too important a function for amateurs: it should be left to the professionals.

Conclusions

As in other countries the strong co-operative movements in Israel are in the agricultural (including rural development co-operatives) and consumer sectors. Despite nationalistic and other pressures, worker co-operatives have not flourished and attempts by the Histadrut to promote industrial democracy in its own plants have so far been almost an entire failure. Worker co-operatives have developed in more or less the same way as similar enterprises in other countries and suffered more or less the same vicissitudes of fortune. Financing, efficiency and managerial competency seem to generate the same problems everywhere. In view of the successes of the Kibbutzim, the Moshavim and the consumer co-operatives, one would have expected great development among worker societies. Daniel says (1976, p. 213) that "the growth of producer co-operatives was due to the needs imposed by reality and to temporary conditions: the ideological base was almost completely missing". Vitales, (quoted in this publication) however, does not attribute all the blame for the slow development of co-operatives to ideology. He says that "associations of this type face special obstacles and are thus difficult to organise". Though this statement was made in 1929 it is still true today. Worker co-operatives are no soft option for the creation of employment even in an idealistic state like Israel.

The Israeli transport co-operatives which are the oldest of their kind in the world have served the country well for many years. Unfortunately, however, their recent development has become rather disappointing. This is very much due to the nature of the business and to the attempts by government to strike a balance between private and public utility. Mergers leading to monopolies became necessary in order to stabilise the industry and make it efficient but consequent government attempts to regulate fares opened the floodgates for high wages and large deficits. The latter had to be covered by state subsidies and higher fares and so the whole process became self defeating. Recent indications are that the transport co-operatives are going through very lean times and may eventually have to be changed into state enterprises.

The most interesting modern development in Israel has been the industrialisation of the Kibbutzim even though these enterprises are based mainly on hired labour. There is a lesson in this for Irish Agricultural Co-operatives. They could go much further than at present in the organisation of rural development subsidiaries like building, drainage, water supply co-operatives, etc., and thus do something about increasing employment in areas where they have been reducing it over the years through capital intensive rationalisation programmes. In many small towns the only industrial employment is provided by the creameries and with several of these closing down, this employment is being discontinued. An attempt should, therefore, be made by the large co-operatives to establish small industries of some kind in the vacated creamery buildings. At first the workers employed could be hired personnel but in any plants which tend to grow, the workers could be asked for a stake and given representation on boards of management. In the long run this might be the best way to establish small industries in rural areas.

Chapter 6

Workers' Co-operatives in Yugoslavia, France, Italy and Denmark

Yugoslavia

Yugoslavia is the best example available of a country with a market economy where practically all enterprises, both industrial and service, are self-managed. For that reason the way it achieved its present structure and its performance under this structure are of interest to our discussion. We look at these factors briefly below.

After the Second World War the system of central planning was followed in Yugoslavia. Under this system the enterprises were planned and managed by the state which was represented in the firm by the director. The interests of the workers were mainly represented by the labour unions under the influence of the government through the Party. As in all centrally planned economies, the free market was abolished and according to Kavcic (1974) non-recognition of the influences of market laws led to harmful consequences in the distribution of goods.

Up to 1948 the country was strongly under the influence of the Soviet Union but friction which had been developing for some time came to a head with the Soviet economic and political blockade in that year. Stalin expected the blockade to break the resistance of Yugoslavia, but Tito was able to mobilise the people to overcome the difficulties. For this, a generally accepted programme was needed and such a programme was the *revival of the free market* under a self-managed system. This came into force by law in 1950. The new system represented a move away from Soviet type centralised control of the economy and a substantial increase in political freedom. According to Jenkins (1973) acceptance of the programme was due partly to an interest in freedom for its own sake and partly to a hardheaded recognition of the merits of a Western-style economy.

Self-management was first introduced in the production sector and some years later in the educational, health and similar institutions. Under the 1963 Constitution a special form of self-management was introduced in government administration, while a further new Constitution, adopted in 1974, extended self-management as an integral social system throughout the whole economy. Over the years the competencies of self-management were enlarged. At the beginning workers' councils were mainly a consultative body of directors. They had very limited powers of autonomous decision-making. Today all important decisions in plants are made by workers directly, or by workers' councils or other self-managerial bodies.

Self-management of enterprises is based on social property (not state property). This property is placed at the disposal of the workers' "collective" which consists of all the employees in the enterprise. The workers are obliged not to diminish the value of the production means or property but to enhance it.

The development of self-management has essentially been a fight against bureaucracy. In communist countries the bureaucracy holding power on behalf of the workers becomes a real governing social class with diminishing influence by the broad masses of workers. Such a social practice differs from the concepts of society given by the classics of Marxism. According to these, the appropriation of political power is the first phase only of the socialist revolution. This phase must be followed by revolutionary changes in the sphere of production relations, leading finally to self-management which, according to Kavcic (op. cit., p.13), is the highest form of communism. We see therefore how co-operation or self-management can fit into different ideologies. Because it uses market forces as a means of allocating resources it is acceptable in capitalistic countries, whereas it is acceptable to communists because the means of production are not owned by private individuals or companies and decisions are claimed to be made by the workers.

Because Yugoslavia is essentially a communist state, one must be wary of saying that their system of worker management is a good example to follow in a mixed economy. As it happened it was introduced as a counter to the Soviet blockade and may thus be considered as a nationalistic movement born out of adversity. We wonder, however, if such a system would have developed in a non-communist country in similar circumstances. By the time Yugoslavia adopted self-management much of the ingredients for it were already there. Private property had been abolished, workers' councils were in existence, at least in name; industry was under state control. The further step to self-management was therefore not so great. In capitalistic countries, on the other hand, the step would be much greater. The real difficulties here would be the abolition of private ownership, a step which would probably be resisted to the ultimate degree. The Yugoslavian example must therefore be taken with a good deal of reserve.

Indeed the reports indicate that the economic situation in that country is not as rosy as some commentators would have us believe. An article in the *Economist* (28/10/1978) says that: (i) incomes are rising much faster than productivity and a total of 600,000 people face the prospect of a drastic wage cut from 1 November 1978. The government's case is that the self-managed enterprises have been over-paying themselves. (ii) Strikes have occurred and are occuring in a number of large enterprises. There were so many in May that it was called "the month of strikes" in the newspapers. All the strikes are about low take home pay. (iii) The limit on the spread between maximum and minimum wages is leading to the emigration of skilled workers and engineers. But in addition emigration of unskilled workers is particularly heavy.

It would seem therefore that self-management has not been the answer to Yugoslavia's economic problems. This must not necessarily be taken, however, as an indictment of the system. Many people would argue that the Yugoslavian enterprises are not really co-operatives at all, that they lack one of the six basic principles of co-operation, namely: open voluntary membership. Furthermore, Yugoslavia has political problems which cannot be solved by any type of free enterprise organisation. Massive government spending on defence is creating budgetary difficulties. The government is taking so much from enterprises in taxes and other imposts that firms have little or nothing left over for investment. Investment funds come, therefore, from borrowing with a resultant increase in the money supply and a high rate of inflation. Inflation is now running at 15 per cent per annum and a large austerity programme seems to be the only solution.

Workers' Co-operatives in France

The first French workers' co-operative was founded in Paris in 1834 by a group of gold jewellers. They were inspired by the philosopher, J.P. Buchez, historian of the French Revolution, who said that "self management can be considered as a Republic in the place of work" (quoted in Steinherr and Vanek, 1974). It was not until 1848, however, that other examples followed and those that did rose from the impetus of the revolution. Of the several hundred associations of workers formed at this stage few survived. Further associations were set up in the 1860s as a result of the availability of soft loans from the government of Napoleon III. Later in the 1880s still more associations were started with the aid of the legacy of a wellwisher. Few of these survived also; the cause of failure lay in the very source of their establishment—the availability of easy access to finance meant that genuine workers' commitment from the bottom was absent.

Later initiatives arose mainly from committed groups of

artisans although some other enterprises were set up following strikes or as rescue operations. Such initiatives have continued over the years so that the total number of French co-operatives has been rising fairly steadily from 119 in 1901 to about 560 today. The growth in numbers was high following both World Wars and during the Depression of the 1930s.

Most of the workers' co-operatives are members of SCOP (Confederation Generale des Sociétés Co-operatives Ouvrièrs de Production) which is the Producer Co-operative Movement's Central Agency. SCOP headquarters has a staff of 25 in Paris with eight more in the provinces. It is financed by a levy of 0.5 per cent on the annual turnover of each affiliated enterprise (Campbell, 1976). The staff gives specialised assistance to the enterprises on financial business and social matters. It advises on the establishment of new producer co-operatives and organises training schemes. A congress of the members is staged every three years in Paris.

There are over 550 SCOP enterprises with some 35,000 members. One-third of these enterprises were founded before 1945 and 11 per cent before 1914. Campbell (1976, *ibid*) states that recent successes have been due greatly to the help given by SCOP and to the goodwill of the French Co-operative Banks (Banque Francaise de Credit Co-operatif and Caisse Centrale de Credit Co-operatif). Also French producer co-operatives are given preference in bidding for certain government and local authority contracts. Whenever a contract can be split into four equal parts, a producer co-operative can opt for one of the parts at the average price agreed with the conventional firm for the other parts.

The majority of co-operatives affiliated to SCOP are rather small enterprises. Average employment in the 300 smallest in 1975 was 12-15 people. More than 80 per cent of the SCOP co-operatives probably employ under 70 people and well over 50 per cent fewer than 15 people. At the other end of the scale, less than 20 per cent employed more than 70 people. The latter included one large enterprise manufacturing telephone equipment which employed about 4,500 people, two building co-operatives employed 1,000 workers each, while a copper wire manufacturing unit and a glass bottle factory had 675 and 500 workers respectively. These five co-operatives are exceptions in terms of their size and the level of technology which they use but they do indicate that co-operatives can become big business and compete successfully with other giants.

Almost half the co-operatives in 1975 were building and civil engineering enterprises. This was due probably to the relatively modest fixed capital needs required for starting such business and to the fact (mentioned above) that public authorities in France assign contracts in such a way as to assist co-operatives. L'Hirondelle, the largest of the construction societies, founded in 1920, built the Hilton Hotel at Orly Airport. According to Oakeshott (1978 p.124) the remainder of the co-operatives were spread fairly evenly between printing, newspapers, services, leather and textiles, glass and "other".

The most unusual co-operatives are the "Service Group" which consist mainly of enterprises started after the Second World War and are employed in activities like town planning, architecture and market research. In Britain and Ireland these would almost certainly have been formed as partnerships or private companies. Other interesting enterprises are the printing, newspaper group co-operatives which includes three large newspapers organised on a co-operative or more or less co-operative basis—*Le Monde* in Paris with a national daily circulation of 450,000, *Le Courier Picard* in Amiens with a daily circulation of 80,000 and *Yonne Republicaine* in the Department of Yonne, with a daily circulation of 45,000. According to Derrick (1979) *Le Monde* was formed as a Société à Responsabilité Limitée on the initiative of journalists at the premises of the defunct *Le Temps* in 1944. It was re-organised on a more nearly co-operative basis in 1968 with shares being held collectively by the journalists to the extent of 40 per cent and the rest by middle management, office and clerical staff and certain outside individuals. The print workers decided against coming in as joint owners. Return paid on share capital is limited to six per cent. Surplus earnings, when available, are distributed to worker members in proportion to pay. The editor is elected by the workers.

Le Courrier Picard and *Yonne Republicaine* are both formally incorporated as co-operative productive societies and affiliated to SCOP and through it to the International Co-operative Alliance. *Le Courrier* employs about 280 people; the print workers are members of the co-operative and have half the seats on the board, but only half the journalists are members. The paper was formed into a co-operative at the end of the war. It ran into difficulties in the 1960s as a result of distributing too large a part of its profits, but under new management it is now prosperous and about to change over to photo composition. The *Yonne Republicaine* was started as a consumers' co-operative and converted to a productive society in 1954. All of the 200 or so workers have to become members after they have completed four years service.[9]

Structure

According to French law seven or more people may start a co-operative which must be controlled by the General Assembly of its members (Campbell, 1976). Non-workers may also become members but they may not compose more than one-third of the management committee which directs the enterprise. This committee must comprise between 3 and 12 members elected annually by the General Assembly. Individual enterprises may, at their discretion, give their members an extra vote for every five years membership. In 1975 non members accounted for as many as two-thirds of the total

[9]During the period when the *Times* newspapers in London were on strike the National Union of Journalists published a study which was cautiously optimistic about changing these papers into workers' co-operatives. Nothing came of the suggestion, however.

labour force in SCOP co-operatives.

The law also stipulates that in the event of liquidation any surplus funds must not be shared out among members but must be passed on to some other co-operative. In this way the law effectively blocks the possibility of outside capitalistic take-overs. There is another important legal provision relating to profit distribution. The workforce as a whole (whether members or not) must receive as large a share of profit handout as that allocated to shareholders in relation to their shares. This ensures that all workers and not just members reap the fruits of any profits made. It has a disadvantage, however, in that it makes workers unwilling to acquire shares since they can share in surpluses without being shareholders.

Finance

All members of SCOP enterprises must contribute at least six months salary to the capital of their enterprise over a period of 10 years. The two co-operative banks service all the enterprises, but they take no more risk than any merchant bank, especially in regard to new enterprises. In 1964 SCOP started a special fund with a levy of 0.1 per cent on the turnover of its enterprises. The total of this fund had reached £400,000 in 1972. Two-thirds of the loans made from the fund, go to existing co-operatives and one-third for the conversion to co-operatives of existing conventional firms. No money from this source is normally made available for starting new ventures.

Conclusion

It would appear that French workers' co-operatives are relatively much stronger than their British counterparts particularly in regard to numbers employed. Boggis, (1973) says that the French experience is an impressive one with growth rates better than national averages and investment outpacing that in private industry. He states that the real progress of the French workers' co-operatives started around

1950 at the same time as a methodical policy of education among the members began to be carried out. It was found, at the time, that the problems which arose in recruiting top rate managerial and specialist staff and integrating them into the co-operatives was a crucial one. Coming to terms with this problem highlighted the educational needs. To aid in this direction SCOP founded the Bilan Co-operatif which provides information on various topics and advises on programmes of economic and technical training for co-operative workers.

The Italian Movement[10]

Italy has roughly five times as many of co-operative enterprises and workers as there are in France. A high proportion of the Italian co-operatives are, however, communist controlled and it could be argued that these are not genuinely independent democratic enterprises; that they are products of the Italian Communist Party (PCI), controlled by the party at the centre.

Italian co-operatives are affiliated to three different associations who represent three different political groupings. The Lega is the communist grouping of co-operatives mentioned above; the Confederation[11] is a broadly Catholic/Christian Democratic grouping while the Association[12] reflects the Republican/Social Democratic opinion. Each of the three groupings include other sectors—agriculture, housing, retail trade, credit and so on—as well as workers' co-operatives. Figures for the latter in 1977 are given in Table 3.

Development of Italian Movement

The earliest record of workers' co-operatives goes back to the 1850s, but substantial development did not occur until

[10]This description of the Italian co-operative movement is taken mainly from Oakeshott, 1978.

[11]Confederazione Cooperative Italiane.

[12]Generale delle Cooperative Italiane.

Table 3: *Italian Workers' Co-operatives, 1977*

	Lega group	*Confederation group*	*Association group*	*Total*
Active enterprises	1,425	1,000	250	2,675
Numbers employed	110,000	32,500	5,000	147,500
Average employment	77	33	20	55

Source: Oakeshott, 1978,

the 1880s. In 1887 the first co-operative federation, namely, the Federazione delle Cooperative Italiane, was formed. Six years later this became the Lega. The number of co-operatives affiliated to the Lega grew from 68 in 1896 to 2,189 in 1916 and to 4,302 in 1921. Most of this growth is accounted for by building co-operatives. Why the overall growth occurred is not easy to pin down but some of it at least must be accounted for by a greater willingness to take on professional/managerial staff than existed in France and also by legal advantages such as those contained in the co-operative law of 1883 which, among other things, granted exemption from stamp duty to co-operatives during their first 10 years. Further legislation in 1889 allowed co-operatives to contract directly for public sector tenders and permitted public authorities to grant co-operatives exemption from the requirement of putting up bonds and signing contracts with them without recourse to competitive tender.

Until 1919 the Lega was the single national organisation of the Italian co-operatives. Following the Bolshevik Revolution in Russian, Italian politics became more polarised and this in turn led to the establishment of a Catholic co-operative grouping in 1919, the Confederation. As a result, between 25 and 33 per cent of the Lega co-operatives seem to have transferred their affiliation to the Confederation. In 1920 the

Lega established formal links with the Socialist Party but in 1925 under a decree of Mussolini it (the Lega) was dissolved. Many Lega co-operatives closed down at this time but a number put their political principles to one side and accepted the new fascist controlled syndicate which Mussolini had established as early as 1921 and which included the Confederation. At the end of the war in 1945 both the Confederation and Lega were again reconstituted and both gained important political achievements about this time. The first, and the key to what happened later, was the inclusion in the New Italian Republic's Constitution of an article (No. 45) indicating that the state will assist by the most suitable means, the development of co-operative organisations. In 1947 formal legislation on the lines of this article was passed. Under the legislation the co-operatives once again were to enjoy most of the privileges of the pre-1914 period along with some new ones. As well as the 10 years exemption from stamp duty, interest on members' capital was exempt from tax. The co-ops were also eligible for special low-interest loans and enjoyed their old exemptions in the matter of bonds and tender procedures. Provincial and local authorities were permitted to grant special treatment to the co-operatives. Among the supervisory restrictions introduced was a limit on the maximum amount of members' capital. It was also laid down that 50 per cent of any co-operatives' profit must either be distributed to members or held on their account for insurance and welfare purposes. In the event of dissolution the co-operatives were not allowed to distribute any net assets to their members—residual assets would have to be devoted to social projects. A further restriction was that a co-operative was not normally allowed to have a membership of below twenty-five, though in special circumstances the minimum was nine.

The third co-operative organisation was formed in 1952 when a minority of co-operatives affiliated to the Lega seceded and established the "Association" referred to earlier.

It seems as if the motive behind the split was political. The Lega had moved very close to the communist party, making republicans and social democrats in the organisation uncomfortable. It would be wrong to assume, however, that the Lega is even today totally communist. In the 1970s the customary distribution of seats on its ten-man Presidential Council has been communists—six, socialists—three and social democrats and republicans together—one.

In most respects co-operatives of the three Italian groupings can be treated as a single species. They operate under the same laws and share the same structures. Sovereign power rests with a general meeting of members. Most workers (rarely less than 60 per cent in an active co-operative) are normally members; only a very small number of non-workers, if any, enjoy membership. The members in general meeting elect a policy-making board. The board in turn appoints the management, a decision which in some cases has to be ratified by the general meeting.

Despite these and other similarities, major differences are exhibited as between the three groupings and between individual co-operatives. The most significant difference between individual co-operatives is their varying policies on capital subscriptions. Capital subscriptions vary from a nominal £5 to the equivalent of three months starting salary in some cases. Under Italian law members may only receive interest on their subscriptions; dividend payments are not allowed. Hence the differences in the subscriptions laid down are not of fundamental importance.

Notes on the Individual Groups

The Association: More than half of the active workers' co-operatives in the Association group are civil engineering and building firms, including the largest single enterprise which employs between 400 and 500 people. There are also a number of building material co-operatives (particularly in marble and other stone-cutting) as well as printing and footwear production firms. In addition there are a number of industrial service enterprises including office and factory cleaners. In recent years also the Association has become involved in job saving operations; one of the Associations credit banks has recently acquired control of a private credit bank in the Ravenna region, while a marble-cutting operation outside Pisa has been successfully converted into a co-operative. However, compared with the scale of the Lega operations, the Association initiatives in this regard are very modest.

The Confederation: Well over half of the Confederation's co-operatives are small and medium-sized building enterprises with the largest employing 400-500 people. About one-quarter are service co-operatives of various kinds, while the remainder are involved in manufacturing. In all sectors most of the co-operatives are small businesses employing about 25 people and it is claimed that they wish to remain thus; indeed their leaders say that independence depends on smallness which is a reflection of true co-operative virtue. However, Oakeshott (1978, op. cit.) states that unless new initiatives are taken, the impact of the Confederation's workers' co-operatives is likely to remain restricted to the world of the small builder. The leaders of the movement are aware of this danger; hence they foresee "conversions of existing businesses" rather than "new start ups" as the answer to the problem. Early in 1958 the group became involved in the conversion of a fairly large textile enterprise in Milan which in its capitalist days employed more than 1,000 people. In March 1978 the co-operative had absorbed 480 of these employees in the new firm. Over 100 other rescue appeals have been received in recent years but the unions have blocked takeovers by the Confederation in all except a few cases. This is a disturbing political situation and one which will have to be resolved if the Confederation is to make progress.

The Lega: The Lega group accounts for a far greater volume of employment than the other two groups put together, and these numbers suggest that one should look to it for the main development potential of the Italian workers' co-operatives. Its principal operations are shown in Table 4.

Table 4. *Lega workers' co-operatives in 1977*

	Number of enterprises	*Employment*
Building and engineering	352	59,500
Manufacturing	315	20,800
Services	758	31,000
Total	1,425	111,300

Source: Oakeshott, 1978.

Like the other groupings the Lega's main thrust is in building and engineering but it also includes a very large service sector. Its enterprises are considerably larger than those of the other groups and from the mid-1970s onwards its building firms have been securing overseas contracts. It has also been pursuing a vigorous and fairly successful policy of rescue operations during the recent depression and has committed itself to an ambitious programme of expansion and development through amalgamations.

In the apparent high success rate of the Lega rescue operations, two factors have been of special importance: access to cheap credit under the privileges enjoyed by Italian co-operatives and the congruence of the Lega's social and political objectives with those of Italy's main communist controlled trade union federation. Evidently its rescue operations have been immune to the trade union hostility which it is claimed has thwarted the Confederation's efforts.

Just as the apparent success of its rescue operations suggests considerable vigour and dynamism on the part of the Lega leadership, so does the move into export markets by consortia of its building and civil engineering enterprises. Its export contract order book is reported to have jumped from nothing in 1975 to £80 million in 1976 and to £150 million in 1977. The most important contracts were secured in Third World countries with socialist inclined ideologies: Algeria, Mozambique, Somalia and Tanzania. It has also worked in overseas environments which are ideologically less sympathetic: its co-operatives formed part of a consortium, alongside private and state-owned Italian enterprises which carried out large building contracts in Iran during the Shah's regime.

To sum up, it can be said that the Lega is a substantial group of co-operatively structured, communist-led enterprises employing well over 100,000 people. Geographically these co-operatives are located in Northern and Central Italy. Industrially they are heavily concentrated in civil engineering and building while in manufacturing their main strength lies in the related areas of building materials and building plant. Of course, as stated at the outset, the real character of the Lega's co-operatives has to be left with a question mark. Nevertheless, if these enterprises are accepted as genuinely co-operative, then Italy has more worker co-operatives employing more people than any other European country. Its progress should therefore be closely monitored by those who feel that the co-operative movement can contribute to industrial development and employment creation.

The Co-operative Movement in Denmark[13]

Co-operatives have been in existence in Denmark for over 100 years. The movement was introduced in 1866 starting with a consumer co-operative in the small town of Thisted in

Jutland. Joint purchasing organisations were soon established and in 1896 they united into a single organisation, The Danish Co-operative Wholesale Society (FDB). Shortly after came the agricultural societies and since then many other fields have been covered. A Central Co-operative Committee was founded in 1899 by the then existing groups of co-operative societies for the purpose of supporting each other generally and to handle problems too big for any individual branch, such as the founding of a co-operative bank, the formation of a cement factory, the co-operative purchase of fertilisers, etc. FDB became a member of this central committee and remained as such until 1972 when it resigned to unite with the Copenhagen Consumer Co-operatives. Today FDB is an independent co-operative head organisation similar to the Central Co-operative Committee which now deals almost entirely with agricultural and other rural societies. A third central organisation, to cater for the workers' co-operatives is also in existence. This is the Central Union of Urban Co-operative Societies (DkF).

In Denmark there is no co-operative legislation and co-operatives register under ordinary company law; accordingly members are free to formulate their own rules. In most cases, however, these rules are very strict. For example, agricultural co-operatives usually have a legally binding contract with members to deliver all of a particular item of produce to the co-operative and to purchase certain input items like fertilisers from it. Another unusual obligation signed by each member, is to cover the present or future debts of the co-operatives. This guarantee is unlimited and personal and operates in most local co-operatives. The obligation to deliver as well as, in

[13] For a more detailed discussion see "The Co-operative Movement in Denmark" published by The Central Co-operative Committee of Denmark, The Central Union of Urban Co-operative Societies and The Danish Co-operative Wholesale Society, 1970. Also Pederson Clements, (ed.) 1977. *The Danish Co-operative Movement.* The Danish Institute, Copenhagen.

some organisations, a similar obligation to buy from the co-operative, together with the joint unlimited liability are special Danish characteristics and it is claimed that they have contributed greatly to the strength and competitiveness of Danish Co-operative enterprises.

As in most countries the co-operative movement in Denmark has attained the greatest importance in agriculture, in the consumer sector, in house building, in insurance and in the monetary field. Approximately 90 per cent of the production of meat and milk is sold through co-operatives which are owned and controlled completely by their members. About one half of all Danish households are members of consumers' co-operatives. The latter in turn are members of The Danish Co-operative Wholesale Society from which they purchase the majority of their requirements, some of them under a "voluntary chain" contract. The accepted ultimate aim, is a National Consumers Society, embracing the whole country and integrating both wholesale and retail distribution.

There are about 600 non-profit house building and house supplying co-operatives throughout the country and the number of dwellings built and owned by these has risen greatly in post-war years. The Danish Co-operative Bank, founded in 1925, is now the fifth largest bank in the country with a network of 300 branches. There is also a Workers' Co-operative Bank for urban workers which is the sixth largest bank in Denmark.

Co-operative insurance societies are also very widespread. All the mutual insurance societies operate on a co-operative basis and the movement has broken into the larger insurance business where it exerts a strong competitive influence. One very large co-operative, The Dairy and Agricultural Accident Insurance Society now covers all kinds of non-agricultural accidents, as well as automobile insurance.

Apart from the above areas, the co-operative form is asserting itself only to a comparatively small degree in the wider industrial field. The large Danish export industries and the many industries supplying the home market have, as a rule, been organised as joint stock companies. Public production and distribution activity in various fields are carried out by the government, the municipalities, or by concessionary companies. This is true of railways, tramcars, buses, ferries, post offices, telephone and telegraph, gas, electricity, water, etc.

The growth in public sector activity has not, however, prevented the extension of co-operative enterprises into a great number of these and other fields, though few of such co-operatives are closed worker societies. Some of the more important of these industrial and development co-operatives are described briefly below.

The Danish Co-operative Cement Factory was an example of a real large scale industry. It was founded prior to the First World War by the Consumers' Co-operative Societies, the societies supplying feeding stuffs to farmers and a number of other cement consuming associations. The objective was to provide competition against the concentrations and monopolistic price policy of the private cement trust. Until 1975 the co-operative produced its own cement but that has now stopped; it now supplies its members with cement bought from a big private company which is the only firm in Denmark still producing cement. The cement co-operative, however, continues to manufacture paper sacks for cement and fodder.

The Co-operative Sanatorium Association is an example of a very unusual and special Danish venture. When the anti-tuberculosis programme was started in Denmark, around the turn of the century, executives of co-operative dairies and consumers' societies resolved to take part in the work. On the basis of small contributions from the members, or per kilo of milk, a sanatorium was built. This sanatorium has now been disposed of because tuberculosis has been practically eliminated, but the association is currently operating a hospital for rheumatic diseases, with substantial public support.

Many small trade groups operate their own co-operative

societies. Fishermen's associations sell fresh and frozen fish and process industrial fish into oil and fishmeal in large factories in Jutland and Bornholm. Gardeners market large quantities of their produce through special co-operative marketing associations. A substantial part of the production of fruit, chiefly apples, is sold for home and export use through these marketing associations.

The increasing use of electricity in Denmark in the early part of this century was for several years based on co-operative power stations. Later on, the introduction of alternating current and the advantages of large scale operations made it necessary to close down the small units. The large stations which today produce electricity are, in some cases public, in other cases, semi-public co-operative associations, but in other cases they are regular co-operatives.

The water supply in many small towns and villages is organised on a co-operative basis also. The same is true of district heat, which has made great strides in recent years. Several hundred co-operative district heating associations have so far been established. There are about 20 co-operative laundries in Denmark. They collect the laundry and bring it back a few days later washed and ironed. In addition there are many co-operative freezers throughout the country which store meat, fruit and vegetables for housewives. Many other examples could be mentioned such as co-operative ferries, plantations, trout fisheries, fire brigades, village halls and even a co-operative theatre which brings high class performances to rural areas.

Workers' Co-operatives

According to Leonora Stettner (1979) Denmark is unique in respect of the relationship there is between the trade unions and the co-operative movements. In no other country, except Israel, is this relationship so close. Since 1907, (when the Nordic Labour Congress meeting in Oslo declared that the co-operative movement should be considered an important instrument in the workers' class struggle) the Trade Union Federation (LO) has seen itself as comprising three wings with shared objectives, namely:

1. To organise workers to bargain with employers for better wages and working conditions,
2. to exert political pressures through the Social Democratic Party with a view to bringing about economic reforms and social security for workers, and
3. to provide a form of co-operative organisation as an alternative to private enterprise through which workers can achieve various economic objectives such as job security, management control, protection of consumer interests, support in the struggle against multinational corporations, etc.

With the objective of co-ordinating and furthering the workers' co-operative movement the Central Union of Urban Co-operative Societies (DkF) was formed in 1922.[14] This is an umbrella organisation whose functions are to represent the interests of the movement to the Government, Parliament and other public bodies, to spread public knowledge and understanding of co-operatives and to provide workers' co-operatives with information and advice on legal, administrative, economic and technical problems. Both the Trade Union Federation (LO) and the Social Democratic Party have seats on the DkF board and DkF is represented on the Economic Committee and the Steering Committee of the Social Democratic Party (Mortensen, 1977).

Currently there are 653 societies affiliated to the DkF and adhering to the standard rules prescribed by it. Of these, 490 are housing societies, 65 are building co-operatives, 49 are canteens; there are 18 bakeries, 5 oil and fuel co-operatives

[14]The current address of this organisation is Det Kooperatibe Frellesforbund, Reventlowsgrade No. 14, Copenhagen 1651.

and 30 miscellaneous societies. Total employment in these societies is about 14,000 workers.

Housing Societies

Though these are affiliated with the workers' co-operative movement, the housing societies might more aptly be described as consumer co-operatives whose ware is housing. Operating on the principle of rentals at first cost they administer over 300,000 flats, more than 3,080 shops and a whole range of shared facilities such as recreation and youth clubs, nursing schools and ball grounds. They employ 3,500 full time and 2,500 part-time workers. A National Building Fund (administered by the National Co-operative Housing Association, the National Association of Tenants, and the Ministry of Housing) makes loans to finance building projects, rent reductions and resident share payments. Its funds are derived from compulsory rent increases and from state loans. Total revenue from rent in 1975 was about 2,000 million kroner.

In order to join a housing society a membership share of 50-100 kroner must be paid. If the member requires a home the additional down payment is three per cent of the cost of the property. Rents depend on the size of flat rented. Households with children have priority to flats of three or more rooms and families with small incomes have priority to the slightly older and cheaper housing. In allocating houses seniority of membership is taken into account.

Building Co-operatives

The National Association of Building and Construction Co-operatives is the apex organisation of the building co-operatives. The first of these was established in 1899 the year of the biggest labour battle in Danish history when 40,000 workers were locked out. Since then they have made steady progress and today the National Association has 65 constituent companies in the fields of contracting, brick-laying, water, ventilation, sanitation, painting, carpentry, joinery and electrical installations. In addition to these it has two architect-engineering planning concerns and a few block-making and kitchen-unit manufacturers which serve all the housing and building co-operatives. The number of dwellings built has risen from 30,000 at the end of the Second World War to over 250,000 today. In all, some 5,000 workers are employed. Some of the building societies have federated and a few operate nationwide.

Canteens

The National Association of Catering Co-operatives originated after the Second World War. At that time workers in large firms wished to control the delivery of and pricing of goods in industrial canteens on a non-profit basis and improve conditions of sanitation. Most of the canteens purchase consumer durables at large discounts for sale to workers as well as some goods for further processing. The 49 member organisations employ 250 workers serving some 20,000 employees. The latter are members of the National Canteen Association, either directly or through their local trade unions.

Co-operative Bakeries

Some 18 bakeries commanding 27 per cent of the bread market and employing 800 workers constitute the National Association of Co-operative Bakeries. Value of sales in 1975 was 192 million kroner. The first of the co-operative bakeries was established in 1894 to break the monopoly of Master Bakers which operated at that time. They started with a share capital collected from workers but today they are organised most often as limited companies in which the trade unions hold shares. The main customers for the co-operative bakery products are the consumer co-operatives but there are considerable sales to other firms. In 1965 the Central Association of Bakeries started a biscuit factory which today has a turnover of 24 million kroner and exports 90 per cent of its production.

Fuel Co-operatives

The purpose of the five fuel co-operatives is to ensure a supply of fuel at reasonable prices to consumers. In 1948 there were 13 fuel co-operatives dealing mainly in solid fuel. Of these only four are now left and they deal entirely in oil products. In 1962 the Workers' Fuel Co-operative in Copenhagen joined Swedish OK-Oil to set up the Co-operative Danish OK-Oil which is now a very large business. It imports oil from the Swedish Co-operative OK refinery and then retails it through some 600 shops mainly attached to consumer co-operatives. Danish OK-Oil and the four fuel co-operatives have a combined staff of 157 and had a turnover in 1975 of 380 million kroner.

Miscellaneous DkF Co-operatives

The 30 miscellaneous societies attached to the DkF employ about 1,800 workers. These societies include an auditing institution, three wholesale dairies, two insurance companies, printing works, newspaper and book publishers (The A-Press), book binding, a computer centre, a project and architect department, purchase organisations, a bank and a workers' theatre. Among these the workers co-operative bank is probably of greatest interest. Set up in 1919 it has as shareholders, trade unions, the LO, the DkF, and individual wage earners. With 36 branches and 700 employees it is now the sixth largest bank in Denmark. The A-Press is also of much interest. It employs 466 people and publishes three daily newspapers with a total circulation of 94,000.

Economic Democracy

Workers' co-operatives are looked on by the labour movement as major instruments for achieving economic democracy. The principles which underwrite economic democracy are written into the constitution or model rules to which co-operatives must adhere in order to become members of DkF.

These principles are of three kinds:

1. those which ensure representation of workers' interests,
2. those which ensure representation of consumers' interests, and
3. the so-called "parity" principle which ensures against speculative capitalistic gains for co-operative shareholders.

Workers Interests

With regard to these, it is laid down that the objective of workers' co-operatives is not to create pockets of "worker capitalists" which would split the interests of the labour movement and alienate the trade unions. It is rather to promote the general welfare of working people and thereby the solidarity of the labour movement. *As a result the trade unions and the co-operatives have agreed on a system of workers' rights based on the principle that every disagreement in a co-operative enterprise should be resolved by negotiation and not through strikes and lock-outs.* It also explains why DkF encourages workers to hold shares on a collective basis through a members investment club or through a federation and not through individual subscriptions.

In primary societies (in which members may be individual shareholders) individual democracy is achieved through the principle of one man one vote. In secondary societies (in which members are organisational shareholders) voting bears a relationship to the number of shares held, but it is stipulated that, in order to avoid domination by any one group, no organisation may exercise more than 40 votes or more than 25 per cent of the total votes. Similarly worker influence on the executive board is safeguarded by the requirement that one-third of the members of the board, both in primary and secondary societies, shall be elected directly by the workers in a separate meeting. The other two-thirds are elected by the general assembly, half to represent shareholders and half to represent consumers or the general public.

Consumer Representation

Concern for the interests of consumers has been a primary motivating force in the development of Danish Workers' Co-operatives, and clauses, relating to the provision of quality goods at reasonable prices, have been written into most of the official documents which made up the constitution of the DkF and the model rules for its members.

Despite this concern for consumers' interests, however, sharp differences of opinion arise from time to time between the LO and the DkF, on the one hand, and the Consumer Co-operative Council on the other. It is reported by Stettner (1979) that at the 1978 annual general meeting of DkF these tensions erupted into open and very sharp debate. The crux of the argument was the accusation by DkF and LO that in its drive to meet competition in the modern world of retailing, the consumer movement had pushed rationalisation and centralisation to a point which seriously threatened member democracy, above all, employment in the DkF industries. This debate is likely to continue.

The Parity Principle

A safeguard against speculative gains is the "parity" principle. Co-operative shares are redeemable only in the event of death, liquidation, or if the shareholder no longer fulfils the requirements of being a shareholder. Permission to redeem can only be granted by the board of the co-operative concerned. The parity principle also states that shareholders may only take out of the co-operative the value of their original investment (with no account taken for inflation). Thus there is no incentive to wind up an enterprise in order to realise the assets which have grown in value over time.

Another facet of economic democracy coming within the parity principle is that shareholders in workers' co-operatives should not be permitted to reap "speculative capitalistic" gains from the workers in the enterprises. This is achieved through the principle of limited return on capital. It is written into the standard rules that interest on shares should not exceed national bank interest plus two per cent. Any remaining surplus, after payment to legal and other reserves, should be used for the co-operative financing fund, or for education, or for such social purposes as holiday funds.

Financial Support for Workers' Co-operatives

From the very early days it was recognised that the capital requirements for industrial co-operatives are beyond the resources of the worker members. Trade unions have, therefore, contributed to the financing of practically all workers' co-operatives in Denmark. In part this contribution is made at the local level by the individual trade unions most closely involved. Primarily, however, trade union finance is channelled through financial institutions at the national level, particularly through the Workers' Co-operative Bank.

Another source of finance is the labour movements' Co-operative Finance Fund (AKF) which was started in 1953 with contributions from the LO, DkF and the Workers' Co-operative Bank. Its purpose is to promote co-operatives through investment of risk capital and to provide a co-ordinating link through its representatives on the boards of the enterprises which it finances. The AKF also provides assessment and monitoring services for co-operatives with the help of economic and financial advisers drawn partly from the Joint Secretariat, the Co-operative Auditing Institute and the Workers' Bank. It operates to some extent like the Management Section of the Mondragon Co-operative Bank in Spain (discussed in Chapter 4).

In 1977 the AKF had assets of 19.9 million kroner of which 77.3 per cent was contributed by trade unions and 22.7 per cent by co-operatives. Some 16.6 million kroner were invested in approximately 40 firms. Of these the construction industry accounted for 77.5 per cent. The loans vary in size from 8,000 kroner in the smallest firms to 3 million in the largest.

Joint Political Efforts

Collaboration between workers' co-operatives and trade unions also takes place at a broad political level. The workers' movement plays a major part in achieving the political aims of the labour movement as a whole. Currently there are a number of issues which are engaging the concerted attention of the various organisations concerned (LO, DkF, and FDB). Since 1973 the workers' movement has been urging the enactment of the *Wage Earners' Investment and Dividend Fund Bill* which would require all Danish employers to pay a prescribed percentage of their wages bill to a fund which would eventually result in a majority of shares being held by wage earners. Under the recent coalition government, however, the emphasis has been shifted to legislation for pure profit-sharing schemes.

Also since 1973 legislation has been under consideration which would give wage earners representation on the boards of all Danish companies as well as strengthening their rights to participate in general meetings. In addition, the LO and DkF are collaborating in a drive to encourage and support worker takeovers of private firms threatened with closure. In this connection they are jointly supporting a bill proposed in 1978 on "Promotion of employment" which would *inter alia* provide state support for such takeovers. There are also legislative proposals envisaged to curb the influence of multinational corporations.

Conclusions

There are certain lessons to be learned from the Danish experience. In Denmark the trade union movement has consistently, since 1907, recognised the significance of co-operatives in promoting the general welfare of working people and thereby the solidarity of the labour movement. The unions have, therefore, contributed to the financing of practically all workers' co-operatives in the country both through the Workers' Co-operative Bank and the Co-operative

Finance Fund. It would be interesting to see the Irish trade union movement channel some of its pension and other funds into co-operative developments, on an experimental basis, to see if employment could be generated through such enterprises. The start could be modest but there should be careful monitoring of results.

On the question of competitiveness there is something to be learned also. The Danish unions acknowledge that the chief prerequisite for the development of co-operation is the maintenance of its competitive position and to this end two points are agreed:

1. Every disagreement in a co-operative enterprise should be resolved by negotiation and not through strikes and lock-outs, and
2. greater demands (concerning wages and working conditions) should not be posed on co-operatives than on private firms (foreword to 1949 Agreement between LO and DkF quoted in Stettner, 1979, p. 95).

These are sound principles which should be kept in mind by unions in all countries.

Chapter 7

*Co-operatives in Ireland**

In Britain in the early nineteenth century the emerging movement of co-operatives and trade unionism were practically indistinguishable. The result was that British co-operatives grew up as a movement of artisans and thrifty middle-class workers mainly occupied in the consumer retail business. During the 40 years following Rochdale, when the British movement was undergoing considerable expansion, there was little co-operative progress in Ireland. When modern Irish co-operation did emerge it did so almost as an exclusively agricultural movement—and as such it has remained (Bolger, 1977, p.1).

Northern Ireland

Co-operative societies in Northern Ireland (as in Britain and in Southern Ireland) can register under two Acts of Parliament, namely:

The Friendly Societies' Act (NI) 1970, and
The Industrial and Provident Societies' Act(s) 1969

The Friendly Societies' Act covers six classes of society, all of which must be charitable and non-trading. These are: (i) Friendly Societies; (ii) Workmen's Clubs; (iii) Benevolent Societies; (iv) Cattle Insurance Societies; (v) Old People's

* In response to requests from readers of earlier drafts we have given somewhat more detail about the overall co-operative movement in Ireland than that given for the other countries listed.

Homes Societies and (vi) specially authorised societies, e.g., Loan Societies.

The Industrial and Provident Societies' Act covers trading co-operatives of all kinds, such as:

1. Distributive (General Supply) Societies, i.e. consumer co-operatives.
2. Agricultural Societies.
3. Housing associations.
4. Miscellaneous societies, e.g., social and sports clubs, self-help/industrial/worker co-operatives and community workshops.
5. Credit Unions.

For a co-operative to become registered under the Industrial and Provident Societies Act, at least seven members plus the secretary must sign the application form and must satisfy the Registrar of Friendly Societies as to the objectives of the society. That is, it must be a "bona fide co-operative society" or a society for the benefit of the community. It must produce a set of rules acceptable to the Registrar as satisfying the legal requirements of the relevant Acts or a set of model rules which have previously been accepted by the Registrar.

For example, the Ulster Agricultural Organisation Society (UAOS) is the officially recognised body for the organisation of agricultural co-operation in Northern Ireland and as such it has sponsored a set of model rules which can be used by all agricultural societies. The Department of Manpower Services has also sponsored the drawing up of model rules for those societies which have been established as community training workshops for young people under the Department's Youth Opportunities Programme (Eynon, 1978). Apart from saving time there is also a financial advantage in using a prepared set of model rules—£35 as opposed to £75 where the latter are not used.

Some statistical information relating to Co-operatives in

Northern Ireland for the period 1967 to 1976 is given in Table 5. As can be seen from this table, there were a total of 83 societies, other than Credit Unions registered under Industrial and Provident Societies Acts in Northern Ireland in 1976 and there was little variation in this number over the 10 years shown. More than half the societies registered are agricultural and about a quarter are housing societies. There were only two distributive societies registered in 1976 but these accounted for almost 80 per cent of total membership in all societies and had sales of £23.7 million which is more than half that of all the agricultural societies combined. There were 14 miscellaneous societies in 1976 with a membership of 11,257 and it is within this group that the industrial workers co-operatives are to be found.

An examination of the Register shows that the following societies can probably be regarded as representing the industrial co-operative movement at present in the province:

Whiterock Pictures Ltd., Belfast
Carn Fasteners Ltd., Swatragh, Derry
Newry and Mourne Co-operative Society Ltd., Newry
Northern Ireland Co-operative Enterprises, Belfast
Bone Enterprises Ltd., Belfast
Edenard Enterprises Ltd., Belfast
Anderstown Co-operative Ltd., Belfast
People's Garage, Avoca Park, Belfast

As part of our study, a number of these establishments were visited and meetings held with people interested in the co-operative idea.

The findings and impressions gained on our visit to Northern Ireland are outlined below, where we present six case studies of enterprises which are different in a number of ways—in the method of establishment, their mode of operation, etc. We then go on to outline the general impressions gained from

Table 5: *Statistics relating to Northern Ireland trading co-operatives 1967-1976*

	Agricutural			*Distributive*			*Housing*			*Miscellaneous*			*All societies*	
Year	*Returns*	*Members*	*Sales*	*Returns*	*Members*	*Sales*	*Returns*	*Members*	*Assets*	*Returns*	*Members*	*Assets*	*Returns*	*Members*
	No.	*No.*	*£m*	*No.*	*No.*	*£m*	*No.*	*No.*	*£m*	*No.*	*No.*	*£m*	*No.*	*No.*
1967	55	24,360	10.0	7	207,497	15.9	16	363	3.9	8	6,818	–	86	239,038
1968	54	24,399	11.1	5	206,385	17.4	16	370	4.0	7	6,776	–	82	237,930
1969	56	25,055	12.3	4	208,779	18.0	17	363	4.1	8	6,760	0.05	85	240,957
1970	55	23,643	13.6	4	215,647	17.9	18	382	4.3	8	7,067	0.05	85	246,739
1971	54	23,484	15.9	3	197,490	17.0	19	395	6.1	9	7,912	0.05	85	229,281
1972	55	22,484	18.0	3	134,442	15.0	18	373	5.1	10	8,440	0.07	86	165,739
1973	52	23,016	19.6	3	134,997	16.0	18	372	5.3	12	8,663	0.10	85	167,048
1974	49	22,744	23.7	3	136,407	16.7	20	400	5.5	14	9,156	0.15	86	168,707
1975	48	23,053	32.3	3	135,097	20.1	20	441	5.5	13	9,864	0.41	84	169,826
1976	46	23,072	43.2	2	133,824	23.7	21	419	5.4	14	11,257	0.24	83	168,142

Source: Register of Friendly Societies (NI) Annual Reports.

meetings with people involved with co-operatives in Northern Ireland.

Whiterock Pictures

Among the co-operatives visited in Northern Ireland was Whiterock Pictures, which is situated in the Springfield area of Belfast. This establishment was set up in 1973 to carry out block mounting. The process involves the purchase of the copyright for prints and the mounting of the prints on to chipboard. The idea originally came from someone who is not in fact involved with the co-operative but who felt he wanted something to be done to help overcome unemployment in the area. A number of people from outside the area seized on the idea and along with some local people decided to set up an establishment which would carry out this process. The idea of a co-operative was taken up because it was felt it would be the best way to get local involvement in the scheme. In an article in *Cope News*, Issue Number 4, Philip Cahill states: "It was never intended to provide employment for a large number of people but designed to show through the employment of a few that self-help could be the answer to many of the communities' problems not only economically but socially as well".

On establishment the co-operative had only one person employed, there are now four people employed full-time along with one person on a part-time basis. The co-operative members include outsiders but while all the workers are not registered members, it is the workers in the co-operative who make all the decisions without interference from outside bodies. As the co-operative is small in size there is little need for formal rules and guidelines on decision making. Regular meetings of the workforce are held to keep everyone informed of the co-operative's up-to-date position. Wage levels are decided collectively, but differentials are decided mainly on the criteria of need, i.e., a married person with a family gets paid more than a single person with no dependents. The co-operative gets some outside help on the management side, while one of the workforce is doing a part-time course on management techniques. Absence of management skills, lack of market research and a shortage of initial start-up capital were the main problems on establishment. The workers were unable to contribute to the setting up of the enterprise as they had been out of work for some time. Eventually the start-up capital was obtained from the Local Enterprise Development Unit (LEDU) which gave a grant of £1,500 and from local subscribers who contributed a similar amount. The latter sum has since been paid back. There is no equity shareholding in the enterprise. It was stated that the internal cash flow was sufficient so that there was no need to borrow from outside even in the short-term. It is hoped that Whiterock Pictures may be able to diversify into new areas following a few profitable years. To facilitate this diversification as well as to advance the present enterprises, it is felt that economic and financial advice rather than direct financial aid would prove more useful.

Carn Fasteners

Northern Counties Co-operative (NCC) is an agricultural co-operative which was set up in 1963 in Swatragh, Co. Derry. It has 2,000 local shareholders. In 1974 a wholly owned subsidiary company called Carn Fasteners was set up to manufacture wood screws. The purpose of this factory was to absorb some of the surplus labour arising in agriculture in the area and also as a community building exercise. It employs 25 people on a three shift basis. This is an interesting development. Seldom do we see agricultural co-operatives becoming involved in industrial enterprises other than in food processing.

Carn Fasteners is not itself a workers' co-operative though some of the workers have shares in NCC. It has experienced few of the problems which the other co-operatives we visited had encountered because it started from a position where a management team was already available in NCC and it had fairly adequate resources available. This, however, does not mean that it can afford to be uncompetitive or sloppily run. As had happened in many instances elsewhere, the members of the parent co-operative would soon close it down if it started to lose money.

Newry and Mourne Co-operative Society

Newry and Mourne Co-operative Society is a local area development co-operative established four years ago. In 1975 the premises of a factory that had closed down were purchased by the co-operative for £100,000 and are now used as an industrial estate for small factory units. The capital was raised through local fund-raising efforts, a grant from LEDU and a loan from Allied Irish Banks. There are now 12 tenants on the estate. Of these four come under the umbrella of Newry and Mourne Co-operative Society, namely:

(a) Glanree Furniture which employs nine people.
(b) Newry and Mourne Development Company Limited which runs the industrial estate, itself giving employment to four security men.
(c) Playway Furniture which manufactures wooden educational toys etc., employing at the time of the interview (May 1978) three people and hoping to expand this to 8-10 people.
(d) Mournecraft, a training workshop, which in May 1978 had three people employed. This was due to go up to 16 immediately and eventually to 85 people, made up of one manager, 12 instructors and 72 trainees. The training is to be provided in conjunction with the Department of Manpower.

The training workshop which the co-operative operates in conjunction with the Department of Manpower Services is an interesting new development.[15] A number of training/

[15]There were 16 similar workshops in existence at the end of 1978.

activity areas were identified and it was then proposed to develop the ability of the trainees to handle tools and materials, as well as developing their general aptitude and interest in specific spheres. Examples of the activity areas include jewellery making, wood carving, pottery, engraving, etc. Trainees are to be given an opportunity of moving from one activity area to another. However, if a trainee shows a particular aptitude for certain activities further training arrangements will be considered. The different activity areas will be introduced in stages with a build-up over nine months to the eventual total of 72 trainees. Each unit operating in a particular activity area will have one instructor and six trainees. It is hoped to make an arrangement with Newry Technical College for day release facilities for the trainees. All details of this scheme had not been worked out when we visited the co-operative so we could not determine how successful it might be.

It is felt that given favourable conditions the co-operative will move into a strong position in the future. While this enterprise is not a workers' co-operative, many of the problems it encountered are similar to those faced by such co-operatives. Its biggest problems initially were in the marketing and sales areas but this has now been largely overcome. The manager believed that many co-operatives suffered from a lack of managerial skills. He also said that co-operative workers needed people to motivate them and to take decisions but such people should not be allowed to become too powerful.

Northern Ireland Co-operative Enterprises, Belfast

This is a co-operative which was involved in the building trade and also had a craftmaking enterprise employing paraplegics. The buildings end of the co-operative was doing badly when we visited Northern Ireland and was on the verge of folding up. The craftmaking part of the enterprise is not commercially oriented, mainly because the people working in it are not as economically productive as fully fit people. There are only three people employed in it at present but approval has been obtained from Government Departments to increase the employment to 12-15 people.

Bone Enterprises Co-operative, Belfast

Bone Enterprises makes playground equipment and also carries out some general light engineering. It was established in 1973 and now has seven people employed. To compensate for its small size it does not attempt to cover a large range of equipment itself but instead carries out sub-contract work for larger firms. The enterprise ran into difficulties from the beginning mainly because those in charge had little idea of business methods and techniques. A number of outside people had therefore to be brought in to help run the firm through a management committee made up of 10 people all of whom are shareholders and only half of whom are from the area. The manager is also a shareholder and there are four other shareholders. It is not a true workers' co-operative in that the workers are not shareholders. There is, however, a profit sharing scheme in operation. Playground equipment was chosen as a product because there was a lack of playing facilities in the area and this started people thinking along the lines of supplying equipment for playgrounds. It has made a profit in only the last two of its five-year existence—although the losses in the other years were not great.

Edenard Enterprises, Belfast

This enterprise was set up in 1973 to make clothes. Clothing was chosen as a product because of a tradition in textiles in the area. The enterprise was established by Roman Catholic clergy to combat unemployment in the area whch had been exacerbated by the political troubles.

Originally the enterprise produced knitwear on four old machines purchased for £500. The knitting was done on a voluntary basis in the evenings and at week-ends to raise money for more machines. It soon became apparent, however, that knitting was not a viable undertaking. The machines were too expensive relative to their capacity and to make them economical would require a three shift working pattern. Due to the troubles this was impossible; night work was too dangerous.

The next move was into a whole-time clothes making industry with money generated from the knitting and with the aid of a gift of finance from a German Archbishop. LEDU was not interested at first because the enterprise was going to operate in the clothing sector which was in decline at the time. It had to start, therefore, without any government grants. Now LEDU has shown its willingness to help and has given the usual 30 per cent grant for new machines as well as a loan. Overdraft facilities are available from the banks. At present the enterprise employs 30 people, almost all of whom are women. This compares with 15 employed in 1975. Wages are similar to those paid in comparable jobs locally. Half the sales are in Northern Ireland with the remainder being exported (only 10 per cent goes to the Republic). To get markets the workers canvassed local firms and shops. They have carried out contracts for the government, e.g., postmen's shirts. Cloth is imported, mostly from Hong Kong.

Edenard Enterprises is a co-operative but is not a workers' co-operative. The manager is a Roman Catholic clergyman. The management committee is made up of the manager with three other locals and two women from the factory. There have been no disputes in the works so far but there were two dismissals for alleged incompetence. The co-operative is in a profit making situation but the level of profitability would need to be raised as the premises are in need of major repairs.

General Impressions of Co-operatives in Northern Ireland

Before visiting Northern Ireland we had been led to believe that there were quite a number of workers' co-operatives in that area. The foregoing notes show that the only enterprise which could be described as a workers' co-operative is Whiterock Pictures and this unfortunately is very small. Workers' co-operatives in that area are therefore not well developed, the so called workers' co-operative are mainly community development enterprises. The most interesting thing we discovered from our visit was that in their training programmes the manpower training service try and locate saleable products and then train people in groups to make these products. We understand that some such groups started as co-operatives but have since been taken over by private enterprise.

Both before and since visiting the Northern Ireland Co-operatives we have had numerous discussions with Mr David Eynon, Industrial Co-operative Adviser with the Local Enterprise Development Unit (LEDU) which is equivalent to the small industries division of the IDA. Mr Eynon's work is of much interest to people in the Republic of Ireland and we describe his functions briefly here.

The role of the Industrial Co-operative Adviser is to "educate, advise and financially assist groups of people wishing to establish industrial co-operative enterprises, to liaise with and act as a catalyst in directing the group(s) and so enable them to prepare adequate proposals for consideration of "government assistance". To enable this stage to be reached LEDU is prepared to give financial assistance to enable a bona fide group to:

1. employ a manager,
2. initiate research and development, and
3. assist with marketing, accountancy, administration costs, etc.

In other words, the Industrial Co-operative Adviser is prepared to examine the pre-development production requirements of any eligible group and make a fairly substantial contribution towards the group's overall costs. He does, however, look for some form of commitment and evidence of ultimate viability of the project.

Eynon tells us that he has recently had a number of encouraging talks with some of the Northern Ireland government training centre personnel with the objective of interesting them in the temporary secondment of skilled instructors to industrial co-operative enterprises. He is also investigating the possibility of establishing a miniature Action Resource Centre whereby the larger Northern Ireland Companies would second one or two of their middle managers for periods of 3-12 months to a co-operative in need of help or advice. Other avenues being investigated include the compilation of a register of available skills amongst retired or semi-retired people, many of whom would welcome the chance of passing on their knowledge and crafts to others and who would be willing to make themselves available on a part-time basis. Eynon sees tremendous possibilities in this idea and he already has lined up a number of very skilled retired people who are more than anxious to train younger groups. Eynon also sees potential for workers' co-operatives in the recent registration of a number of community training workshops on the lines of that organised by the Newry and Mourne Co-operative Society described above. At the end of 1978 sixteen such groups were formed under the aegis of the "Manpower Service Youth Opportunities Programme Scheme". Of these eight were registered under the Industrial and Provident Societies Act while at least two had been registered using the ordinary Companies Act.

At a recent meeting dealing with co-operative organisation in Magee College Derry, Eynon, 1978 (op. cit.) stated that in his view the conversion of existing businesses to co-operatives could represent the best way forward for the industrial co-operative movement. It overcomes many of the fundamental problems which affect the embryonic worker co-operatives and can, if promoted properly and skilfully, show the movement in a new and better light to the general public. He went on to say that many successful businesses, especially small family businesses, are often faced with the problem of having no one in the family who is competent to take over the running of the business. In instances of this nature, the possibility of converting to a co-operative can offer the most agreeable solution to the existing family shareholders and the workers.

The acquisition of money by the workers to purchase the shares of the firm is the difficulty here. In many cases the cash should be obtained from a local bank but in general some type of co-operative bank is needed for such financing: Eynon says that "There is a very strong feeling amongst people involved in industrial co-operatives that the establishment of a co-operative banking facility is absolutely crucial if there are to be worthwhile developments in the future growth of these societies. The very word 'co-operative' can bring alarm to the eyes of ordinary agencies responsible for the lending of capital and with some justification when one examines the past history of industrial co-operatives."

Republic of Ireland

The modern co-operative movement in Ireland is generally accepted as dating from 1889 when the first co-operative creamery was established at Drumcollogher, Co. Limerick. Prior to that, elements of co-operativism were to be found in the operation of the Irish clan system and amongst small communities where the land was sometimes on a collective basis.

Horace Plunkett saw the need for Irish industry to be organised on an efficient basis. Competition from imports from British colonies and the mass production techniques of British industry coupled with the development of cheap transport by the railway system had a damaging impact on Irish agriculture and industry.

Co-operative stores were tried originally, but later Plunkett concentrated on the dairy industry. After many efforts had failed he succeeded in getting the Drumcollogher creamery started. Five years later, in 1894, there were more than 30 such co-operative creameries. In that same year, the Irish Agricultural Organisation Society was founded.

In addition to establishing creameries, Plunkett and his colleagues also formed Societies for the supply of farm inputs (seeds, fertilisers, etc.) and for the marketing of farm produce. The Irish Co-operative Agency Society Ltd. was set up in 1893 and achieved some success in marketing butter and supplying creameries and farmers with dairy requisites. In 1897 the Irish Agricultural Wholesale Society—a new federation of agricultural and dairy societies—took over the agricultural supply area.

Agricultural credit societies, on the lines of the German Raiffeisen Credit System and similar to the present-day credit unions, were established around this time also. These credit banks did much to help farmers break out of the cycle of indebtedness to merchants, which forced them to sell their produce at low prices and buy inferior goods at exorbitant costs. By 1908 there were 268 of these banks and though the money handled was small, with the maximum loan being only £50, they performed a useful function. The banks declined during the years of the First World War although some survived up to the late nineteen thirties.

By 1908 there were 881 co-operatives (over one-third of them creameries) with a membership of 86,000 and a turnover of £2.25 million. Between 1914 and 1920 the number of co-operatives rose from 1,023 to 1,114; membership increased from 106,000 to 158,000 and turnover from £3.67 to £14.6 million. The early 1920s saw a decline in fortunes. The Ulster Agricultural Organisation Society was set up in 1922 with a consequent loss to the Irish Society of 141 co-operatives and 15,000 members. The economic slump, the civil war of the 1920s and the world depression of the 1930s resulted in a fall in the number of co-operative stores from 300 in 1919 to only 83 in 1940 (IAOS, Annual

Reports for various years).

It was not until the 1950s that things again picked up and as agriculture developed so too did the agricultural co-operatives. By 1974 there were over 200 agricultural co-operatives with a membership of over 180,000 and a turnover of £800 million.

Summary statistics for both agricultural and non-agricultural societies registered under the Irish Industrial and Provident Societies' Act (other than Credit Unions) in 1976 are given in Table 6. As can be seen from this table there were a total of 614 co-operatives registered under these acts in that year. Of these, 243 were classed as agricultural, (153 production and 90 distributive). Of the remaining 371 societies, 203 were public utilities and 86 miscellaneous societies. These numbers would seem to conflict with Bolger's statement, that Irish co-operatives are almost exclusively agricultural, but if we look at the sales or income figures, we see that the agricultural societies accounted for £1,139.2 million compared with only £33.6 million for all the others. Furthermore, a number of the miscellaneous group are community development societies which include some agricultural schemes like deep ploughing and drainage enterprises. Also a large number of small societies were formed, in recent years, to organise group water projects, and are likely to go out of existence when the water schemes are completed.

The table shows that the 118,269 shareholders in agricultural production societies had £11.6 million invested in their co-operatives, or an average of about £98 per member. The average investment per member in the agricultural distribution co-operatives was about £91 per person. Investment by members in non-agricultural co-operatives averaged less than £17 per head. On the whole, therefore, investment per member is very small, being much less than the amount borrowed by the societies from banks and other lenders.

Practically all of the co-operatives registered in the state are affiliated either to the Irish Co-operative Organisation

Table 6. *Statistics relating to societies registered under Irish Industrial and Provident Societies Acts, excluding Credit Unions, 1976*

Type of co-operative	*No. of co-ops*	*No. of share-holders*	*Sales or income*	*Profit or (loss)*	*Liabilities*				*Assets*
					Due to shareholders	*Due to depositors*	*Due to overdraft*	*Other*	
	No.	*No.*	*£'000*	*£'000*	*£'000*	*£'000*	*£'000*	*£'000*	*£'000*
Agriculture									
Agricultural production									
Dairying	72	89,263	825,327	13,254	7,831	7,979	90,565	75,470	228,056
Meat processing	15	12,680	155,459	(3,452)	2,868	2,648	10,375	25,651	44,281
Livestock breeding	39	9,128	10,946	146	343	890	809	1,987	6,627
Horticultural crops	11	3,254	9,260	614	289	321	454	929	2,742
Other production (a)	16	2,944	3,800	(113)	281	577	1,181	1,967	3,587
Total Agric. Production	153	118,269	1,004,792	10,449	11,612	12,415	103,384	106,004	285,293
Agricultural distribution									
Agricultural supply (b)	44	16,540	103,802	1,482	1,504	2,420	5,876	24,864	40,355
Eggs and poultry (c)	4	649	20,280	3	119	185	734	5,032	6,935
Livestock marts	42	62,511	10,310	2,130	5,626	493	3,888	2,382	23,183
Total Agric. Distribution	90	79,700	134,392	3,615	7,249	3,098	10,498	33,278	70,473
Other									
Other distribution (d)	18	14,628	23,247	1,017	1,080	337	375	2,857	5,996
Public utility (e)	203	17,325	898	(3)	300	–	5,840	1,771	7,616
Promotional development	45	87,551	1,170	24	112	–	277	574	988
Fishing	19	2,317	5,645	50	194	33	792	420	1,730
Miscellaneous (f)	86	17,139	2,629	779	633	5,458	372	–	9,388
Total other	371	138,960	33,589	1,866	2,319	5,828	7,656	5,622	25,718
All societies	614	336,929	1,509,702	15,930	21,181	21,341	121,538	144,904	381,484

Notes:
(a) Other agricultural production includes flour milling, chocolate crumb, potato and vegetable production.
(b) Supplies manures, seeds, implements and general agricultural supplies.
(c) Depots for collection and marketing of eggs and poultry.
(d) General stores.
(e) Societies founded to enable members to purchase houses, building plots and group water schemes. Does not include main building societies which are registered under 1874 Building Societies' Act.
(f) Miscellaneous includes clubs, educational associations, workers' co-operatives, regional development, home crafts, publishing, etc.

Source: Report of the Registrar of Friendly Societies for year ended 31 December 1977–Department of Industry, Commerce and Energy, Dublin.

Society (ICOS) or the National Co-operative Council (NCC) or to both. The ICOS, (formerly IAOS) which was founded by Horace Plunkett and his associates in 1894, caters mainly for agricultural co-operatives but recently, it has more and more been including non-agricultural societies in its membership if they are from rural areas. The NCC, which was founded in 1954, caters mainly for more urban type co-operatives, which it was felt at the time could not be admitted to the ICOS because they had no agricultural connection. Nowadays, however, the NCC includes in its membership a number of rural development and fishery societies. The NCC does not publish a list of its membership but it caters for about 40 societies *in toto*. Lists of the various groups of societies affiliated to the ICOS, including the number of members in each group (where available) are given in Table 7 below. As can be seen from this table there were 410 co-operatives affiliated to the IAOS in 1976 out of a total of 614 for the state as a whole.

There are a number of advantages in being affiliated to one or other of the larger organisations, but because it is much longer in existence and more highly developed, the ICOS tends to provide the better service. Some of the services provided by it are as follows:

1. It supplies prospective co-operatives with its general rules and advises them on how to get established and registered as a co-operative. It also provides a legal service to advise on rule changes and other legal matters.
2. It provides a representative service which organises co-operatives into different groups and supplies each such group with a secretary who will represent it at government and EEC committees and makes applications for EEC grants.
3. It provides a management service to advise members on business and financial matters and negotiate with unions on their behalf.

Table 7. *Number of co-operatives affiliated to the IAOS in 1976*

Type of co-operative	*No. of co-ops*	*No. of members*	*Type of co-operatives*	*No. of co-ops*	*No. of members*
Multi-purpose dairies	55	88,261	Crafts	5	9,393
Livestock marts	43	32,811	Livestock breeding	4	42
Meat processing	6	42,180	Gaeltacht	15	5,087
Wholesale	2	260	Miscellaneous	18	4,277
Agricultural stores	31	16,140	Group water schemes	99	n.a.
Horticultural	7	4,039	Other	99	n.a.
Fishing	11	892			
Pig fattening	15	5,071	*Total above*	240	n.a.
			Total IAOS	410	n.a.
Total above	170	189,654			
			All societies	614	336,929

Source: Irish Agricultural Organisation Society Ltd., Annual Report 1977

4. It provides a member development section to educate members on co-operative principles, conduct of meetings, etc.

The ICOS is a member of COGECA, the central organisation for agricultural co-operatives in the EEC, the Confederation of European Agriculture, the Plunkett Foundation for Co-operative Studies and an Associate Member of the Federation of Agricultural Co-operatives in the UK. It is not a member of the International Co-operative Alliance (ICA).

Worker Co-operatives in the Republic of Ireland

While the tradition of co-operatives in the agricultural sector has been strong in Ireland the same cannot be said of industrial workers' co-operatives. At present there are only four real industrial co-operatives in the state, most of which are quite small in size. Total turnover of these co-operatives in 1977 was about £2 million and total employment about 130 people. Here we briefly outline the history of these four enterprises and then go on to discuss some other co-operative efforts in the non-agricultural sectors which are of some interest in their own right.

Graphic Arts Co-operative Society, Dublin

This is the oldest existing workers' co-operative in the Republic of Ireland. It is engaged in printing work such as process engraving. In 1956 a group of craftsmen in the printing industry—platemakers and artists decided to form an enterprise which was to be owned and controlled by the workers. This enterprise got off the ground in 1959 after three years spent in raising funds from the workers concerned to finance the operation. No financial aid was received from any outside body. Initially Graphic Arts employed four engravers and an apprentice. Since then its employment record has varied—going up to 23 people in the 1960s after another process engraving firm was taken over, and declining again to nine people at present. The decline in employment came about mainly because of changes in technology in the trade. All members of the co-operative have one vote regardless of the amount of money each has invested. All the workers have shares although people could work without being members. There are also three members not working in the co-operative. Since 1963 there have been few, if any, new members. The management committee is made up of 12 people, at least four of whom must be working in the co-operative. Four members retire each year on a rotational basis but they are eligible for re-election. The management committee is the governing body between Annual General Meetings and the short-term day-to-day decisions are taken by a manager who consults with the committee.

The Graphic Arts Co-operative is unique among the workers' co-operatives in Ireland in that it was established from the start as a co-operative. The other worker co-operatives were formed by the workers in an already existing firm which was about to close down.

Crannac Co-operative

Crannac Co-operative in Navan is the most widely known workers' co-operative in the Republic of Ireland. This enterprise, which is involved in the manufacture of furniture, was established in 1972 as a co-operative after the firm had gone through a period when it had a number of different owners. The last of these decided, in 1972, to liquidate the assets and close down even though the firm was making a small profit at the time. At this stage the workers occupied the factory for a period of 13 weeks. During this time money was raised from the workers and local people, along with a loan from Foir Teoranta. Foir Teoranta, (a state-sponsored body), was established in 1972. Its main function is to provide assistance for industrial concerns which may be in danger of having to close down, or suspend activities, because of inability to raise necessary capital from commercial sources. The factory was purchased with the available funds. The co-operative now employs 43 workers, compared with 30 workers when it was set up originally. Five of the present staff are women. Each of the original workers contributed £200 to the co-operative, but subsequent workers have only to buy a minimum £5 share. The maximum equity which any member can own in the co-operative is £1,000 and dividends are limited to five per cent per annum. A worker who is leaving may have his equity refunded. The normal source of short-term finance is the bank, where overdraft facilities are available.

The management committee is made up of nine people, three of whom are outsiders. Three members retire annually, but are eligible for re-election. A general floor meeting is held after each committee meeting to notify decisions and generate ideas for new proposals. The committee appoints the general manager, who is responsible for the day-to-day operation of the business. In the early years of the co-operative the general manager and the sales manager were hired employees, not members of the co-operative. After a time both of these were replaced by co-operative members, who seem to be running the operation capably.

In its first years of operation Crannac made a wide variety of furniture, ranging from office and school furniture to household suites. With the onset of the depression in 1974, demand for the former type of furniture slackened off and the firm was forced to concentrate on high quality household furniture, for which it had developed a reputation. Despite this specialisation, the years of the depression proved extremely difficult, particularly for a new co-operative trying to make its mark in a capitalistic environment. During this period the firm sold its output to wholesalers and retailers and not directly to consumers. Under this arrangement, however, it was difficult to keep going. Demand was not buoyant and competition from other manufacturers was exceptionally keen. The staff rose to the occasion, however, and in many instances worked long hours to complete "rush" orders for the peak trade at Christmas and Easter.

Despite this dedication, however, it proved difficult to remain viable in the circumstances. The wholesale/retail mark up was exceptionally high, making the furniture very expensive for the ordinary householder. As a result Crannac decided, in 1976, to go into the retail trade itself. When this happened retailers refused to take its furniture and now it sells all output directly to customers, both in Ireland and in a shop which it has established in Glasgow. The change has proved successful.

The co-operative is a member of the CIF[16] pension scheme, paying a small sum per week for each worker, in addition to the state contributory stamp. The co-operative has had no industrial relations troubles so far, but the employment of a few members have been terminated. Decisions to sack workers have to be approved by the other workers.

General Questions

With regard to some general questions relating to co-operatives, the manager of Crannac thinks that small units are essential if good industrial relations are to be maintained. He thinks that the maximum size for his type of operation is about 100 employees. He does not believe that co-operatives are any more efficient than ordinary well-run businesses, but they certainly tend to be more efficient than badly-run firms where there are union troubles. He would like to see a few successful co-operatives emerging so as to give encouragement to the whole co-operative idea.

When asked about the advantages which co-operatives had over private enterprises, he said that co-operative workers are more aware of the economic forces at work around them than workers in private industry. As a result they will work hard if required. Generally they also have more commitment to the business than private industry workers.

[16]CIF = Construction Industry Federation

The main disadvantages he sees in organising co-operatives is the difficulty of getting the idea across and he is not hopeful about starting new co-operatives except in cases where existing capitalistic firms fail. The raising of capital for starting co-operative enterprises in Ireland at the moment is difficult. There are no specific institutions for this purpose. Foir Teo is there for the purpose of rescuing firms which are in trouble. It does not provide capital for new firms starting off. The IDA could provide money for the establishment of industrial co-operatives but it has little experience in this area. The manager believes, however, that if sufficient viable co-operatives could be got going they would create their own momentum (Vanek's critical mass theory).

Irish Springs, Dundalk

Irish Springs, Dundalk which manufactures spring units for beds was established as a workers' co-operative in 1973, when the previous owners of the firm decided to close it down, after three years unprofitable working. When it was closed the workers occupied the premises for nine months. At the start there were 25 people involved in the sit-in but by the end of nine months the number had dwindled to four. Among these was the present general manager. During the occupation, however, those involved were not idle. They collected money from local people, purchased wire and other raw materials and continued to make springs which they sold (though with some difficulty) to former customers. In order to establish the co-operative, finance was raised through a loan from Foir Teoranta. They also got a grant from the IDA. The premises in which the work takes place is not owned by the co-operative —it is rented from CIE.

A worker is eligible to become a member after a trial period of three months. There is, however, a fairly high turnover of workers. Since the co-operative started in 1973 about 30 people have left for other jobs or have been dismissed. These have been replaced by other workers. The present staff consists of 33 people including the manager. All workers are union members and receive standard union rates for the type of work they do. There are no restrictions on wage differentials. Workers do, however, receive bonuses at Christmas and Easter and interest free loans for the purchase of houses and cars.

The management committee consists of four directors, one of whom is the manager. The three others are outsiders who gave help and guidance when the co-operative was being established. This committee meets every two months or when required. There is also a works council, which meets from time to time to advise the manager on various matters relating to working conditions, wages and distributions of surpluses. The works council is made up of five people elected every year by the workers.

With regard to general questions the manager felt that any single co-operative should not employ more than 100 people and that there was need for an outside overseeing body to look after, advise and finance co-operatives. He did not think that co-operatives were more efficient than ordinary businesses and while he did feel that co-operatives were likely to develop only from desperation situations it was also his opinion that they could play a part in Ireland's future industrial development. There would always be firms getting into trouble and the establishment of co-operatives was a means of rescue. Also under conditions where people had houses and were reluctant to move to other areas, then the co-operative movement might be used to provide them with jobs convenient to their homes. Two advantages which co-operatives have over capitalistic enterprises is that generally members will work hard if required and will not normally go on strike. The disadvantages of co-operatives are that it is difficult to borrow capital and few workers have themselves any cash to invest. The dilemma of collateral is very real. Members are also unwilling to have money stopped from wages to buy shares and it is difficult to dismiss bad workers.

Castle Shoes, Dundalk

This co-operative was formed in 1971 when it purchased the assets of a private company which had been put into receivership. In order to establish the co-operative, a subscription of £50 each was to be paid in weekly instalments by workers formerly employed in the firm. Loans were also obtained from local businessmen and members of the community. In addition a loan was obtained from Foir Teoranta while bank overdraft facilities were negotiated. A local priest, Fr G. Campbell, was the prime mover in the formation of the co-operative. He was also associated with the formation of Irish Springs.

Since its formation in 1971 Castle Shoes has been through a very difficult period. The shoe industry has been badly hit by the elimination of tariff barriers and has had to face strong international competition. The firm has, however, managed to stay in business due to the generosity of local people who have upped their share subscriptions considerably and who have advanced loans and trade credits. Workers have also contributed by being prepared to go on short-time on numerous occasions.

At the end of 1976 the Register of Friendly Societies shows that 3,833 shares at a nominal value of £5 each had been issued to 96 people giving a total equity figure of about £19,000. Of the 96 shareholders, 14 held shares to the value of over £1,000 each while the remaining 68 had holdings of less than £100 each. Employees' subscriptions to date amount to a further £3,248. Many of the employees who had subscribed are no longer with the firm. The workforce in 1976 was 25—15 men and 10 women.

The present manager is an employee of the co-operative. His salary is set by the chairman-secretary of the Board which is made up of the original seven registered co-operative members who do not work in the factory. Most decisions are taken by the manager although there is a more open policy on finance than in a private enterprise. Not all of the 25 workers are shareholders but every worker has a vote in electing six worker representatives to the management committee.

Bewley's Experiment

Bewley's, a well-known company owning a number of coffee houses, restaurants and a bakery in central Dublin, employs 400 people in seven departments. The company is an old and well established family-owned concern. In 1926 it was registered as a limited company, almost all of the shares being owned by the family and a small number by members of the staff. In 1970 the family decided to transfer ownership of the firm to a trust, which would hold the shares on behalf of the company staff. (The total estimated capital value of the enterprise is about £1 million.) On 13 December 1972, after spending some eighteen months working out the legal details of the transfer, the Bewley Community Ltd. became a member of the ICOM movement and was registered as a company limited by guarantee. Being a guarantee company it is non-profit making and any unused surplus is devoted to some social object. If it were wound up or sold the funds would then also go to some social needs and this effectively prevents anybody from selling the enterprise for personal gain. A board of trustees administers the trust and they ensure that any actions of the company do not depart from the spirit of its articles of association; they have the right to veto any action which they feel so departs.

There are nine trustees—three chosen by the community from among the staff, who may not be directors; three chosen by the directors who must be directors; and three from outside the company chosen by agreement between the community and the directors. Contrary to popular belief the company profits have never been very large, but whatever surplus there is, is divided as follows:- 20 per cent or so is given to the staff in the form of a bonus, while a similar amount is made available for social needs in society. The remaining 60 per cent is retained profit and is ploughed back into the firm.

Members of the staff with at least three years service are entitled to membership of the community. A council exists and is composed of the heads and either one or two elected representatives of each department, depending on size. It meets monthly and can discuss any item which is of interest at that time. Both the agenda and minutes of meetings are published and representatives report back to their various departments. Though the council has no legal powers of decision under the articles of the company, it has increasingly played a most important role in deciding on matters within the company and this role will continue to grow with time.

At present the board of directors continue to nominate themselves, as was the traditional way in the firm. Though the desirability of participation was stated in the articles of association it was felt that no specific forms such as worker election of directors should be included, thus giving a more flexible approach. In the case of elections to the board it was felt that initially such a step would achieve nothing. Instead the managing director advocates change by growth and sees involvement growing gradually; this will eventually include election of directors by the members of the community. Indeed at present the community members of the board of trustees sit in at directors' meetings and this could be seen as a precursor to elections.

The Bewley scheme is unique in Ireland and cannot be put forward as a model for widespread adoption no matter how desirable it might be. It takes a lot of courage to give away a firm because you honestly believe that the workers who keep it going deserve it more than you, the person who inherited it. It might be better to put it forward as an ideal rather than a model for the future.

Clover Meats Ltd., Waterford

Though it was decided to omit agricultural co-operatives from the scope of this study, there is one such firm which should be mentioned because it now incorporates a certain level of worker co-operation in its management. This firm is Clover Meats in Waterford. Clover is the second largest co-operative meat producer in Ireland, slaughtering pigs, sheep, lambs and cattle. It produces a variety of bacon and beef products for export and for home distribution. Between 1972/73 and 1974/75 Clover accounted for 21.3 per cent of total national pig slaughterings and 13.5 per cent of total national cattle slaughterings. In recent years, however, it has run into rather serious financial and administrative troubles. The attempts to overcome these difficulties are of interest because of the involvement of the employees and the participation which they now have in the policy-making of the firm.

Background to the Clover Problems

Unlike dairy plants, where the raw material is fairly perishable, meat factories can draw their inputs from a wide area. Meat producers, therefore, are not tied to a co-operative in the same way as are dairy producers, and can readily switch from supplying one meat plant to another if they so wish. This ability to switch supplies can cause serious problems for a meat co-operative. Because it is a co-operative it may be forced to pay above average prices to its members during a glut period, when private plants are paying rock bottom prices. In a period of scarcity, on the other hand, it has to pay full market prices for supplies and even then it may not always be able to get sufficient stocks. The upshot of this is that a private firm can amass reserves in a glut period to tide it over a period of scarcity. The co-operative, on the other hand, cannot do this to the same extent and may therefore get into trouble when supplies slacken off.

The trouble at Clover Meats was in part a reflection of the above mentioned problems. During the 1974 cattle crisis, when prices at marts reached rock bottom levels, Clover did not make as much profit as its competitors. It was thus in a worse position than the others to overcome the problems which occurred in 1975 and 1976 when supplies became scarce and expensive. Added to this was the fact that Clover, because of the location of its main plant, had higher costs (mainly higher distribution costs) than other enterprises in the meat industry. However, there were other factors which contributed to Clovers' weak position—factors inherent in its own structure and in its operations in the preceding decade.

Between 1967 and 1975 Clover Meats diversified very rapidly, acquiring Donnelly's the Dublin bacon factory in 1967, Clonmel Foods in 1968, Lunhams of Cork in 1971 and O'Keefe's in Dublin. National Proteins was built in Waterford in 1972 and in 1969 Associated Irish Meats, a marketing firm based in London was bought. Most of these firms were experiencing difficulties at the time and the bacon industry itself was being rationalised. It also bought a 40 per cent share of Waterford Cold Stores and installed new plant and equipment in all its acquired premises.

These acquisitions were achieved mainly by debt financing. By 1976, working capital requirements were £2.7 million and fixed capital £4.7 million. These requirements were financed by long-term loans of £1.6 million, short-term loans of £3.9 million and a cash flow of only £1.9 million.

At this stage efforts were made to improve the situation by re-organising the management staff, disposing of unprofitable assets and initiating a share capital drive. These efforts, however, were not very effective, partly because shareholders in Clover were losing interest in pigs to the point where only 10 per cent of 400,000 pigs being supplied to Clover came from shareholders. The position deteriorated further during the following year and by Spring 1977 bank indebtedness stood at over £10 million and it looked as if the firm would have to close down.

At this point, following government promptings, a rescue package was drawn up which, among other things, emphasised earlier decisions to get rid of unprofitable plants and press ahead with a share capital drive. It was proposed that £1 million be raised from the sale of assets and a further £1 million through share capital from farmers and other co-operatives. In pursuance of these policies Lunhams in Cork, O'Keefes in Dublin and some land holdings were sold. Clover Meats in Limerick was closed down and the share drive was stepped up. The latter yielded £800,000 which was close to the amount required but to make assurances doubly sure the workers in the three Clover plants at Waterford, Clonmel, and Wexford committed a further £120,000 in share capital. This was to be raised over a two-year period at a rate of £2 per week from male workers and £1 per week from females. In all 700 workers out of a total of about 1,000 agreed to contribute. The number of farmer shareholders is 8,840.

The proportion of shareholders to employees in each factory is:

	Number of workers	*Number of shareholders*	*Percentage of shareholders*
Waterford	625	430	69
Clonmel Foods	200	124	62
Wexford	120	107	90
Management	42	42	100
Total	987	703	71

As part of the rescue package also a council of 60 members was elected by the following groups:

Farmers	34 members
Employee shareholders	10 members and
Other co-operatives	16 members

Of the employee members four are from Waterford, two from Clonmel, two from Wexford and two from office staff shareholders. The council has a number of sub-committees dealing with different aspects of policy but in addition it elects an executive committee of seven members, made up of one worker member, two members representing other co-operatives and four farmer members. Two further members may be co-opted at the discretion of the executive. The executive committee meets regularly to monitor progress and make decisions about general policy matters. The workers' representative is a very active member of the executive but another of his functions is to keep workers informed about the running of the firm without, of course, revealing information which might be of value to competitors.

The development at Clover Meats is a very interesting experiment in worker participation and so far it seems to be working very well. The main thing is to keep the workers fully informed of what is going on so that a "them" and "us" situation does not develop. The workers representative told us that when he came on the Board, workers had little knowledge about the running of the firm and in particular of the difficulties in procuring supplies when national stocks were scarce. They were thus inclined to feel bitter about lay-offs on the latter occasions. One of his main functions now is to inform workers about the stock situation so that they can appreciate the difficulties faced by management and understand why lay-offs and short-time may be necessary.

At first the farmers were rather reluctant to have worker members on the council and they might not have accepted such a revolutionary innovation except for the immense difficulties in which they found themselves. Now that the situation has occurred the farmers seem to accept it without concern and those whom we interviewed were quite enthusiastic about the idea. They felt that the workers were now much happier than heretofore and had a deep concern for the welfare of the firm. Of course here again the workers' attitude may be coloured by the fact that their jobs were in jeopardy a short time ago and they are thankful for their reprieve. With a prosperous firm the idea of workers' representation on the Board might not have been so exciting. However, there are many who now believe that the Clover

Meats experiment will be copied by all other co-operatives for the purpose of having a contented work force with an interest in the welfare of their societies. So far a few other agricultural co-operatives have agreed to worker participation but to date few details of these are available. The Irish Co-operative Organisation Society, however, is pressing ahead with this idea. In a recent document entitled "Framework for Co-operative Development" (1979) under a heading "People in Co-operatives", the Council of the ICOS suggested that "the co-operative objectives need to be reconciled with the aspirations and objectives of the people directing and working in the co-operative movement".

Towards this end the document stated that "the 18,000 employees of the co-operative movement have a major influence on the nature and degree of development that is likely to be achieved. They should therefore be able to identify with the co-operative, seeing it as a true extension of the community of which they are part. Accordingly, special emphasis should be given to:

1. A strong personnel development function within co-operatives designed to meet the obligation on the co-operatives to develop to the fullest extent of their aspirations.
2. Support for staff in applying the co-operative approach, to meeting their needs in particular, through the formation of housing co-operatives, credit unions and other service co-operatives.
3. Ensuring that each member of the staff has a sufficient understanding of the relationship between the member and his co-operative to be a worthy ambassador of the co-operative.

The co-operative movement should seek to ensure that the excellent record of industrial relations is maintained. Accordingly, attention should be given to ways and means in which the co-operatives can take initiatives to this end."

To the cynic these statements may appear to be just lip service to an ideal. And, indeed, in many cases little if anything will be done to have them implemented. However, as a result of discussions with members of the Council of the ICOS we are convinced that there is a genuine desire among the majority to put these sentiments into practice. These members have come to realise that many agricultural co-operatives are co-operatives in name only and that something must be done to change this orientation. Indeed a strong drive in this direction has already begun.

Community Development Co-operatives

There are a number of Community Development Co-operatives providing comprehensive services throughout the country. The activities of three of these: Glencolumbkille, Co. Donegal, Chois Fharraige, Co. Galway and Chorca Dhuibne, Co. Kerry are described below. Space does not allow us to describe several others which are also of much interest.

Glencolumbkille Co-operative

The first co-operative efforts in Glencolumbkille started in 1954 with the arrival in the district of Fr James McDyer. He is quoted as saying, shortly after his arrival, that unless something were done, the end of Glencolumbkille was in sight (Sweetman, 1972). In order to revitalise the area, Fr McDyer set about improving the social and economic life of the area on five bases (Kent, 1977), farming, small industries, home crafts, tourist development and fishing.

The first accomplishment was the building of a community hall in 1956. In 1959 an electricity supply was brought to the area against opposition from the older people who thought it would be too dear and too dangerous. Some time later the local water supply was improved, a new primary school was built and a health clinic was set up.

The first efforts on the economic front were in the agricultural sector with the establishment of Errigal Co-operative in 1961. This co-operative was started with £20,000 share capital subscribed by locals and by interested people throughout the country and abroad. It was to provide advice and raw materials (fertilisers, feeds, tools, etc.) at cost price to farmers, as well as to encourage commercial vegetable growing in the district to supply a local processing factory. An Foras Talúntais was called in to survey the soils in the area and found that only four per cent of 160 acres proposed were entirely suitable for vegetable growing. On top of this local farmers were somewhat reluctant to engage in production; they had no experience of such crops. Despite these difficulties the processing factory opened in 1962 with the help of Erin Foods who owned 50 per cent of the share capital and who were also responsible for the running of the plant and marketing the produce. Over 135 acres of produce were grown in the first and second years (mainly potatoes, cabbage and carrots), but the project was never a success. Nineteen sixty four proved a bad year for crops; 15 acres of cabbage and 12 acres of carrots were lost and most other crops had poor yields. Afterwards local production fell because of lack of confidence, and supplies for the factory had to be brought from East Donegal and Galway thus incurring very high transport costs. The factory had to close down in 1974.

In 1965 the co-operative started a hill farming scheme which provided credit facilities, a pool of machinery and technical aid for hill farmers with the help of government grants. A further scheme to amalgamate land in the parish into a large unit fell through. In 1958 an attempt was made to introduce industry to Glencolumbkille. With the help of Gaeltarra Eireann a factory to make handwoven tweed was set up in 1958 employing about 15 people. This was not a co-operative. It worked reasonably well for a time but when power loom tweed started to replace the handwoven product in other factories the Glencolumbkille effort came under severe pressure and was forced to close in 1973.

In 1964 a handknitting co-operative was established with share capital from housewives. This co-operative is still in operation. Most of the output is exported to England and the USA. A number of other attempts were made to establish co-operatives in the building area and also in hatmaking, but these ventures were not successful.

Tourism was an untapped potential source of income for the Glencolumbkille area. Efforts to enhance the attractiveness of the area included the building of a folk village showing the various styles of past housebuilding in Donegal. A tourist shop and a teashop provide a source of income at the folk village. Between May 1st and October 1st six women are employed in this venture. In 1967 a holiday village, with 20 thatched cottages was built, (not formed as a co-operative). Five women were employed during the winter while two more were employed during the summer. The cottages are usually booked out from mid-May to mid-September, at Christmas and from St. Patrick's Day until after Easter—five and a half months out of 12. Fr McDyer hopes to extend this occupation to seven months by organising various functions such as an archaeological week, a short-story week, etc.

A machine knit factory was also set up in 1967 on a joint venture basis between local co-operative shareholders and a private enterprise. By the end of 1974 this factory had run into debt. It was decided at this stage to buy out the private enterprise and to begin work again with a much reduced workforce. It now employs 27 people.

In 1971 an overall development co-operative was set up with the amalgamation of the Hand Knit Co-operative and a small metalcraft co-operative. The latter had been established when a silversmith was brought to the area and provided with premises. The development co-operative was formed with eight people. Its purpose was to bring development to the area and provide jobs rather than wait in vain for the local people to make jobs for themselves. A local hotel was purchased by the development co-operative with money borrowed from the banks, and the Handknit Co-operative. In 1973, 26 per cent of the hotel was sold to Gaeltarra Eireann. Five people are employed in it all the year around and about a dozen schoolchildren are usually taken on during the summer. Before the vegetable processing factory closed in 1974 a fish processing factory was set up. The factory is owned by a consortium of Donegal Fish Ltd., Comhlucht Siuicre Eireann Teo., Gaeltarra Eireann and Errigal Co-operative. Employment varies from 25 in the valley season to 110 people during the four peak months. The factory concentrates mainly on processing shellfish, especially crabs, and the blast freezing of mackerel, herring and salmon.

In 1974 a shop was rented by the co-operative in Dublin to sell Irish crafts including those from the Glencolumbkille area. The shop also serves as an enquiry agency for both the hotel and the holiday village. In 1976 a craft centre was set up in the premises of what had previously been the Hand Weaving factory. The craftsmen—a silversmith, two weavers, a leatherworker, a metalworker, a potter and a woodcutter are not paid by the co-operative, but they are provided with their premises and some tools.

New developments which Fr McDyer hopes to undertake are:

(a) The setting up of a good restaurant in the holiday village with a wet-day room in the restaurant.

(b) A laundry to wash linen for the hotel and cottages as well as for outsiders. The linen is changed three times a week in 34 cottages and there are 20 rooms in the hotel.

(c) A building co-operative employing local people to do local building and repairs.

Undoubtedly, the efforts of Fr McDyer and those involved with him have been of tremendous advantage to the area. In order to achieve this success, however, the co-operative element has had to be played down because the response from the local people was not always forthcoming. Part of this problem arose because many of the people who contributed to the co-operative's share capital could not play an active part in its operation as they were living outside of Glencolumbkille. The present development is very dependent on one single person and when he goes it will be difficult to replace him. We hope that time will see the development of some type of corporate body which can carry on regardless of personalities.

Comharchumann Chois Fharraige

This is a local area development co-operative in the Galway Gaeltacht established in 1972. It was founded to provide work and various services for the district of Chois Fharraige, the Gaeltacht and the Irish language. By 1979 Comharchumann Chois Fharraige was engaged in eight separate activities, namely:

1. The organisation of Irish speaking summer colleges
2. A printing section
3. A publishing service
4. Temporary schemes such as drainage and group water installations
5. A boat building and repair scheme
6. Production of an Irish magazine (the continued publication of this work has been in serious doubt for some time)
7. A turf cutting scheme
8. The selling of office supplies and stationery to local businesses.

The co-operative has over 400 shareholders and employs 49 people on a full-time basis as well as a number of part-time workers.

Comharchumann Forbartha Chorca Dhuibne (West Kerry Development Co-operative)

Corca Dhuibne is an area about twenty miles by ten in the western half of the Dingle peninsula in Co. Kerry. The present population is about 4,000 people. Traditionally small farming and part-time fishing have been the chief means of livelihood in the area. The land, however, is poor and as a result incomes have been very low. As might be expected emigration from the area has been heavy and in the late 1960s it appeared that a number of small communities were on the verge of extinction.

It was against this background that a group of farmers and teachers in the area got together and decided to do something for the district by getting the people to help themselves. As a result, Comharchumann Forbartha Chorca Dhuibne was started in 1967 as a community co-operative concerned with both social, cultural as well as economic aims. Unfortunately co-operatives had a history of failure in the area and so there was at first a great deal of cynicism and resistance to the idea. As a result many difficulties were encountered in the early years; managers left and it looked as if the co-operative would go out of business despite a management Gaeltacht grant which lasted for five years.

At the beginning, the co-operative was not involved in any mainstream activity. It tried to develop the social and cultural life of the area and to this end built two community halls for plays, dances, meetings, bingo sessions, etc. In 1969 a change of fortune occurred when the co-operative became involved in running Irish language courses. This provided an inflow of income to the area as local people provide board and lodgings for visiting students. Between 1969 and 1978 the number of students grew from 700 to 2,200.

The co-operative commissioned a land survey of the area in early 1970. It was obvious that much of the land needed to be reclaimed if it was to be made productive. Around this time a vital discovery was made. It was found that 12 to 20 inches under the ground there was a hard thin metal plate or putty layer. If this was broken, so that the sub-soil and top soil could be mixed, the land would become fertile and richly productive.

A special swamp bulldozer and a deep plough, similar to the type used for moisture purposes in Italian vineyards, was purchased. More than 8,000 acres of land have been reclaimed in the past eight years. About half of this land was reclaimed by deep ploughing, the rest by conventional means.

This reclamation has had remarkable consequences. One in every three farmers in the area have increased the size of their holdings by an average of 16 acres. As a result of this and of price increases generally, farm incomes have risen dramatically and new and improved farm practices have been introduced. These developments have generated a new confidence locally.

New developments include a two-acre glasshouse, a demonstration farm and the growing of vegetables. A publishing company produces a regular bilingual community newspaper. There are now 32 full-time workers in the co-operative.

Future plans hinge on a share drive to raise £500,000. Most of this will be raised outside the area. This plan includes a cultural centre, an enlargement of the glasshouse, the purchase of more reclamation equipment, costing almost £0.25 million and an indoor sports centre. It is also hoped that by 1980 the co-operative will employ 60 full-time workers. Some of these new jobs will be in a proposed new vegetable processing plant and a small computer firm.

Despite early set-backs the West Kerry Development Co-operative has come a long way in 12 years but it still has a long way to go. If the area is to continue to remain a Gaeltacht much more attention than at present must be given to cultural activities. Social activities also require attention. Far too many young people are leaving because of lack of social life. Further economic developments are necessary also. Cottage industries could be fostered, the surrounding seas could be harvested to a greater extent than at present; overseas tourists could be catered for. There is no end to what could be tried and the co-operative hopes to keep trying.

Other Co-operatives

In addition to the large creameries with a turnover of over £300 million in 1976 other co-operative societies in the Irish Republic at the present time are: 360 credit unions, scattered throughout the whole country; seven home industries, of which the most successful is Irish Country Markets, made up of 48 local produce markets, and Slieve Bawn in Strokestown, Co. Roscommon. There are twelve co-operative fishery societies dealing mainly in fish marketing and eight horticultural co-operatives dealing in fruit and vegetable production, processing, and marketing. There are also twelve co-operative pig producing co-operatives with sales of £5 million in 1974 out of a total pig output in that year of £63 million. Co-operative meat plants account for over 50 per cent of total slaughterings, while there is a co-operative insurance firm, Farm Business Developments Ltd. (FBD) with 25,000 clients and a premium income of over £2 million. There are also a number of housing co-operatives and a large number of group water co-operatives.

Many of the community organisations have been set up as co-operatives not so much because of a commitment to co-operation but rather because a co-operative form of organisation was seen as the best vehicle for obtaining state subsidies. For example, group water co-operatives are bodies set up for the purpose of awarding of state grants for water installation. Without a commitment to the co-operative ideal these organisations become defunct once the purpose for which they have been set up has been accomplished. This is unfortunate as the lessons learned from working together are lost when the co-operatives are disbanded.

Concluding Observations

This chapter shows that the development of industrial

workers' co-operatives in Ireland, both north and south of the border, has been on an extremely small scale. In Northern Ireland, where there is a fairly strong industrial base, one would have expected some progress, but somehow very little has happened. It is true that, from time-to-time, public-spirited people have tried to establish co-operatives but very little has come of their efforts. Either they themselves were not sufficiently enthusiastic or the people were too apathetic. Certainly the Basque spirit was missing; or else there was no Father Arizmendi around to channel political and religious ideas into a co-operative ethic.

In the Republic of Ireland we have been essentially a rural society and the idea of establishing workers' co-operatives for the creation of employment has seldom been considered. If a person wanted a job he thought in terms of emigration to Britain or the USA. It was a simple expedient, and except in times of heavy depressions could be expected to provide a solution to his problem. With jobs freely available abroad and with no language barriers it was much easier to emigrate than go to the trouble of trying to create a job at home.

All this is changed now, however. Jobs abroad are no longer plentiful and it seems that from now on we will have to create our own jobs or go without. But why bother with co-operatives when jobs in private enterprise are much easier to organise? In 1978 the IDA established about 400 small enterprises promising about 5,000 jobs. Why not continue with this work and forget about co-operatives?

The answer is simple. Despite the IDA's most impressive record there is still a great deal of unemployment, and every means of reducing it must be tried. The IDA should, of course, continue with its Small Industries Programme and even step it up if possible. But the co-operative movement should also be exploited. Our investigations have shown that there are many areas where employment creating co-operatives could be established. The areas concerned and the strategies which might be adopted are discussed in the next chapter.

Chapter 8

Discussion and Conclusions

Having discussed the principles and practices of the co-operative system, outlined its theoretical advantages and dis-advantages and reviewed the historical development of the system in a number of countries, we must now discuss the questions posed in the introduction to this study.

Mounting Level of Unemployment

According to many writers part of the pressure for workers' co-operation comes from the supposition that it is able to protect or create employment. How far is this justified? Vanek in *The Participatory Economy* (1971, pp.151-152) says that one of the most critical problems of western style economic development is that of large scale unemployment and lack of job opportunities. In a liberal (western-style) situation where unions tend to keep wages at a relatively high level and employers counter this, as well as losses from strikes, by displacing workers through mechanisation, there is need for some system which concentrates on employment creation. The co-operative seems to have a comparative advantage in this regard. If well organised it can attain its objective without any distorting side-effects on the ratio of capital to labour. It can, if required, adjust its wage levels to competitive levels and in addition it can avoid losses from strikes and other industrial actions.

Another writer, Richard Fletcher (1975), in a draft paper*

* Paper submitted to the British Labour Party Policy Committee.

put forward for consideration by the British Labour Movement in 1975, says that in many areas of our economy "the market is incapable of matching productive capacity to human needs. The most important example is housing where at least a million new homes are needed immediately, while several million more require bathrooms and other simple facilities. At the same time, 750,000 workers are unemployed.

Fletcher goes on to say that the concept of production for use through co-operative organisations should be better able to match needs to human resources. Already the government, through social welfare payments, is paying workers to be idle. With a relatively small increase in payments the same workers could be engaged in socially useful employment creating real wealth.

It can, of course, be argued that the formation of co-operatives is no more than a stop-gap solution in times of crises and that most of them will disappear again when economic conditions improve. On the basis of past experience in these islands this is a fair comment, but we can also say that stop-gap solutions are fully justified during deep and prolonged depressions. Any system of organisation which helps to create viable employment in difficult times is worthy of support. But there are some who believe that the outlook for co-operation is more promising now than at any time in the past. Fletcher (*ibid.*) argues that the economic weakness of the producer co-operatives was largely a function of their position in the historic time-scale, and that under present economic conditions—where it is becoming more difficult to create full employment—their outlook could be very different. The co-operatives' main advantages are their supposedly excellent labour relations and most important of all, their ideology, stemming from the fact that there is no outside owner creaming off the fruits of the workers' labour.

Industrial Unrest

Writers on the subject of workers' co-operatives usually

state that one of the main advantages of co-operatives is their excellent labour relations. In practice very few days are lost in co-operatives due to strikes and on the basis of this behaviour it is argued that co-operative organisation of industry would ensure industrial peace. All students of industrial relations would not, however, accept the latter view. There is now definite evidence that strike proneness is a function of the size of business. Prais (1978) has shown that strike incidence falls dramatically with plant size and on the basis of this evidence we could conclude that the good record found in co-operatives may be due to their small size rather than to any other factor. Prais goes on to say that if there are enough people in a single plant and if its operation depends on all of them being at work, then this fact must inevitably lead to an unacceptably high degree of strike proneness in very large plants. He says "the bigger the crowd the greater the chance of a fight", and this fundamental sociological principle in essence provides a simple explanation of the increased strike proneness of large plants which is illustrated by the data in Table 8.[17]

If large size is conducive to increased militancy and alienation then large co-operatives are likely to be subject to the same stresses as any other large business and there is some evidence to this effect from the Mondragon Co-operative in Spain. As mentioned above, a strike did occur in one of the larger plants there which demonstrates the near impossibility of establishing adequate channels of communication within large organisations of any kind. As a result of this strike the Mondragon thinkers have decided that in future the maximum size to which a co-operative should be allowed grow is around 400-500 employees.

Despite the above analysis by Prais and work in the same

17. Sociologists do not all agree with this simple explanation by Prais. Some of the recent contributions to the literature suggest that the relation between size, morale and militancy is very complex and requires much further study (Newby, 1977, Curran and Stanworth, 1979).

Table 8: *Measures of strike proneness in Britain by size of plant, 1971-1973**

Plant size (employees)	*Percentage of plants with strikes*	*Number of strikes per plant per annum*	*Working days lost per plant per annum*	*Working days lost per 1,000 employees per annum*
11-24	0.2	0.0014	0.3	15
25-99	1.0	0.010	3.7	72
100-199	1.0	0.032	21.5	155
200-499	6.1	0.078	101.4	329
500-999	14.3	0.205	498.0	719
1,000-1,999	25.2	0.368	1,539.0	1,128
2,000-4,999	44.0	0.827	5,744.0	2,075
Over 5,000	75.8	2.478	29.400.0	3,708
All Plants	2.2	0.031	108.0	878

* Manufacturing industry in Great Britain.

Source: Prais, S.J., 1978. (*ibid.*)

area by other writers (see also Shorey, 1975 and Turner, 1969) we are of the opinion that for any given sized firm the co-operative has a better chance of having industrial peace than private or state enterprises. Also, a strike in a co-operative is not likely to spread throughout the economy to the same extent as in other enterprises. However, co-operative management cannot afford to be complacent in this regard. Because human nature is what it is there are bound to be rows when any large group of people are working together. A group of workers will withdraw its labour if by doing this it thinks it can improve its position or inflict hardship on a rival group. Hence problems of industrial relations can arise in all organisations and as firms get bigger, well equipped personnel management teams must be provided, even in co-operatives.

Inflation

Workers' co-operatives have sometimes been thought of as a means of overcoming inflationary pressures. To be effective in this role the whole economy would need to be co-operatively organised, as otherwise the labour managed sector would be dominated by events in other sectors. Secondly, the co-operatives would need to be worker-owned and not just worker-managed. Indeed worker management on its own is described by Oakeshott as being "almost bound to be a recipe for extra inflation" (*New Statesman*, 25 May 1979). Without a stake in the business, workers are not overly concerned with investment which they do not own and are inclined to go for short-term gains in the form of higher wages.

Inflation is not caused by wage increases alone. Many other factors are involved which are outside the control of individual firms or even governments in small economies. It is in maintaining employment in times of depression and high inflation that co-operatives have an advantage, rather than in preventing inflation. Worker owned co-operatives can maintain employment in these circumstances by adopting wage restraint policies and remaining viable when their private sector competitors are forced to close because their employees are less willing to accept such policies or because owners find it more profitable to close down than stay in business.

There is no evidence to suggest that workers' co-operatives can be a powerful weapon against inflation. We saw in Chapter 6 that Yugoslavia, which has a complete labour-managed economy, has not eliminated its inflationary problems.

Efficiency

Evaluation of the efficiency of workers' co-operatives is complicated by various problems. Studies usually try to compare performance of co-operatives with that of comparable capitalistic firms but in such cases the appropriate level of aggregation is not always clear. Should the comparison be between all co-operatives and other firms in an industry/area or should it be on an individual paired firm basis. There is also the difficulty of securing data from both sets of firms at a similar level of aggregation and finally, there is the question of appropriate criteria. What indicators are equally useful in comparing success, either between co-operatives and other firms or even among co-operatives? In view of these problems reaching definitive conclusions on this matter is very difficult. However, the results of recent research suggest that performance of co-operatives—when measured in various ways and by various procedures—has not been nearly as bad as many have contended. Indeed in some cases co-operatives appear to have out-performed capitalist firms (Jones, 1978).

In a comparative study of Israeli kibbutz and similar type organisations, Melman (1969) found that according to various efficiency criteria the co-operatives were more efficient than conventional organisations. This was clearly the case with respect to capital productivity, profit per worker, and labour productivity, with little difference in comparative administrative costs. More recently Barkai (1977) calculated that between 1954 and 1965 the annual rate of growth of total factor productivity for the kibbutz co-operatives averaged 6.2 per cent, significantly higher than for the Israel economy as a whole during that period.

In 1973 Jones (1974) undertook a variety of exercises bearing on labour efficiency in long established British workers' co-operatives. No obvious difference between the co-operatives and similar other type firms was discerned. In general, while labour productivity comparisons support the charge of alleged poor discipline in co-operatives, unit labour cost comparisons do not point firmly one way or another and information on restrictive labour practices and strikes suggest better performance by the co-operatives.

One of the specific weaknesses seen by some (including the Webbs) in the co-operative structure is that workers' co-operatives are usually unable to undertake technical change and that the more participatory co-operatives are the least innovative. Preliminary evidence from the Jones (1974) study suggests that the views of the Webbs are usually mistaken. There is evidence that traditional co-operatives in, for example, footwear manufacture can undertake technical change and that technical change and degrees of participation are positively correlated. But with long established British printing co-operatives, the views of the pessimists are supported: during the 1948-68 period technical efficiency in these firms deteriorated.

In examining the performance of American Plywood Co-operatives Bellas (1972) found a strong relationship between performance (defined as the total return to an average worker over a certain period, plus the net change in the book value of his shares over the same period) and participation. For traditional British co-operatives, however, when money income was used as a yardstick of performance Jones found co-operatives to be, on average, inferior to comparable capitalistic enterprises. An important component of income is non-monetary income and apparently the non-monetary element of real income in co-operatives represents a significant part of total income. However, since it is difficult to measure non-monetary income objectively no clear-cut answer is available as to performance per worker in terms of real income as between co-operatives and other firms.

When the ability of the co-operative movement to grow and form new co-operatives is examined, again no simple answers are as yet ascertainable. The traditional British and American movements, for example, appear to register disappointing performances by this token, but a contemporary form of British Co-operatives (i.e., the ICOM) is enjoying much more success, as is also the Mondragon movement in Spain. The record of the French and Italian co-operatives is also one of growth, though at a much slower rate than that achieved in Mondragon.

The position in Yugoslavia seems to be the least satisfactory. In a study of the efficiency of the co-operative movement in this country up to 1970 Kamusic (1970) found that the position was reasonably satisfactory though he did conclude that capitalistic type businesses (particularly in the developed countries) were more efficient than self-managed enterprises in Yugoslavia on the grounds that:

1. Management in co-operatives is weaker than in other firms.
2. The system of self-management does not always encourage new investments, although co-operatives with high value-added tend to allocate a reasonable proportion of income to reserves. Those with low value-added, on the other hand, cannot afford new investment and therefore tend to become under capitalised.
3. Surprisingly stimulation of workers and professionals is less effective in an average Yugoslav enterprise than in an average capitalistic one, though Kamusic adds that this should not be taken to mean that a self-managed enterprise could not be the most effective form of enterprise in stimulating workers.

Since Kamusic wrote this in 1970 the position seems to have worsened considerably. Millar (1978) says that in early March 1977 about one-third of the labour force in the Yugoslav co-operatives were employed in enterprises running at a loss. As a result wages have had to be reduced to a guaranteed minimum level, insufficient for a decent living under Yugoslav conditions. One result of this situation is to force workers to take on additional work, and a 1976 report claimed that almost 3 million out of the 4.7 million employed in the co-operatives had supplementary sources of income which were in some cases much higher than those in their regular jobs (*ibid.*, p.280).

In summary then, the situation regarding the efficiency of co-operatives *vis-á-vis* other forms of organisation is unclear. Certainly some of the gloomy prognostications have been made too hastily. Sometimes co-operatives seem to have done better than capitalist firms and some evidence exists to suggest that success is positively associated with participation. But the performance of co-operatives is uneven and much additional work must be done before definite conclusions can be reached.

Motivation for Establishing Co-operatives

Our research has tended to show that co-operatives generally are children of distress; distress due to failure of existing enterprises or to failure of an area or region to develop economically. In most societies people do not look outside the realm of orthodoxy, in this case private enterprise, unless that approach appears to be failing. Thus co-operatives tend to arise because the more usual capitalist method is not providing a solution, or when a trade or industry is on the decline. Other co-operatives are formed to fulfil some religious, political or philosophical ideal. Still others are formed in regions suffering deprivation as the only suitable means of generating enthusiasm and motivation among the people.

The Mondragon movement is a prime example of the latter

type of co-operative. The region was broken politically, socially and economically as a result of siding with the vanquished in the Civil War. Private enterprise was unable or unwilling to provide sufficient employment in the area. The absence of unemployment benefits at the time the first co-operative was established made the problem of unemployment all the more pressing. Alongside the unemployment problem, which people wanted to overcome, there was a temendous local pride and a desire to show that the region could stand on its own feet. The co-operative movement was seen as a means of tapping these motivations and providing a proper outlet for them by allowing participation by workers in their own enterprises.

In Yugoslavia and Israel also, it took rather peculiar circumstances to bring the co-operative movement into existence. In the former country the movement was introduced to counter the Soviet blockade of the late 1940s but even at that time private property had been abolished and industry was already under state control. In Israel the co-operatives were closely associated with the Zionist movement and with the desire of the Israelis to found for themselves a permanent home. This was certainly an idealistic experiment.

Traditionally France has been regarded as the Western European country where workers' co-operatives have achieved the greatest success and where the movement is least ideologically rooted. Nevertheless, the French co-operatives are closely allied to the left wing political front which has a strong commitment to a "Republic of the Workshop". In Italy also, the co-operatives have mostly a political or religious motivation. In addition, there is some suspicion that, at least one of the groupings is not a real co-operative movement at all. Despite these suspicions, however, it can be said that the Italian movement has made tremendous progress in recent years and may well form the model for future co-operative development in other countries.

In Britain (and indeed in many other countries) the fortunes of the co-operative movement have been closely associated with the ups and downs of the business cycle. Traditionally the working people have turned to co-operation as a form of self-help in times of economic crisis, in the depression after the Napoleonic wars, in the 1850s and 1890s and after the First World War. The present resurgence of interest in workers' co-operation is rooted in the wave of closures, amalgamations and redundancies associated with the rationalisation and re-structuring of British industry in the 1960s and 1970s. During this period rank and file trade unionists became progressively less willing to negotiate redundancy agreements as they realised that alternative employment was not available. Co-operatives were sometimes chosen as an effective means of fighting redundancy rather than the traditional strike which, if anything, helps rather than hinders factory closure.

Potential for Co-operative Enterprises in Ireland

We now come to the question of the potential in Ireland for new enterprises (both industrial and service) based on the co-operative structure. If previous development of workers' co-operatives in the UK and Ireland were extrapolated we might expect societies to remain restricted to a relatively small number of industries, where the economies of large scale production had not yet penetrated, and capital investment was less important than skilled labour in producing the final product. In this situation the limitation of the field of activity would be such as to make the prospect of establishing viable co-operatives a very gloomy one. There are, however, some more, encouraging features which should be mentioned.

Many people believe (Boggis, 1973) that in future years basic industry will be less important as an income and employment generator, while the service sector will grow. In this situation there would be wider scope than at present for the development of workers' co-operatives since service units are more easily organised and usually require less capital than manufacturing firms. The expansion of the service sector is already an acknowledged fact in developed countries. In the United States the following have shown high employment growth rates: direct mailing advertising, duplicating and copying, services to dwellings and other buildings, research and development laboratories, testing laboratories, business management consulting, equipment rental, coin operated machine rental, repair, photo-finishing laboratories, interior decorating, sign painting, auctioneer's establishments, telephone answering, and supplying temporary help for businesses. Many of these might not be so relevant for Ireland but quite a number of them would and these could easily be developed into small co-operatives.

Co-operatives could also flourish in the business of sub-contracting for construction firms. More and more builders are becoming administrators who take out contracts for jobs but have the work done by small sub-contractors, such as block-layers, plasterers, interior decorators, painters, electricians, plumbers, tilers, carpenters and so on. Any small group of skilled and unskilled people could set themselves up as co-operatives in one or more of these areas and make a very good living in the sub-contracting business where capital requirements would be minimal.

There is scope also for the development of industrial co-operatives in the existing food industry. We have mentioned earlier the move to worker representation on the Board of Clover Meats and other agricultural co-operatives. This movement could be developed further by having other food plants introduce similar schemes or perhaps organise full-scale workers' co-operatives in some of their plants. The formation of the Tuam Potato Processing Co-operative provides a good opportunity for the factory workers to combine with the farmers in the formation of an agricultural/workers' co-operative. It has also been suggested that there is scope for co-operatives in certain large companies which have perennial labour problems. Murphy (1970) says that the Dublin bus service should be broken up into co-operative groups who would rent the buses from CIE and operate them under a franchise from the latter authority. Each group would cover a given area of the city and provide a reliable service on a profit-making basis. CIE would maintain the buses in mechanical fitness and charge a rental which would cover the costs of this service. Such a development might help to promote more harmonious labour relations, end labour troubles and reduce substantially the government transport subsidy, which is now becoming oppressive.

In view of Israeli experience with transport co-operatives, however, we would be reluctant to recommend this course of action here. If it came about, the government would have to be involved in regulating fares and once this happened there would be immediate demands for subsidies. The latter situation might therefore be worse than the former. However, there might be possibilities for CIE and other state-sponsored bodies to transfer ownership of certain subsidiaries to co-operatives of their workers. In view of the industrial relations record of some of these bodies any hiving off of activities should be welcomed.

Another suitable area for co-operative development is in under-developed rural districts where the whole community needs to be organised if economic development is to be achieved. There is a tremendous scope in these regions for co-operatives on the lines of Chois Fharraige, Chorca Dhuibne and those in other western areas. For instance, local people could come together to build tourist cottages, organise camping and caravan sites, establish community centres for the entertainment of children and adults, and even erect cheap hostels for young visitors. Other areas of community development would be the taking over of bogs for peat cutting, the development of stone quarries and sand pits for the provision of building materials and the establishment of co-operative teams of workers to build houses, drain land and fell timber in state forests. The range of activities which could be initiated is almost unlimited.

Most of the above suggestions all relate to the potential for establishing co-operatives where no enterprise existed previously. As mentioned earlier, in the section dealing with Northern Ireland, there is also scope for the conversion of existing viable private businesses and companies to co-operatives, and indeed this could prove to be the most productive method of establishing co-operative societies. In the past many co-operatives were established as a result of the closure of private firms and while some have proved successful, we feel that this is not the most appropriate way of building up a co-operative movement.

To summarise this section we can list the following as potentially likely sources for workers' co-operatives in Ireland:

1. New industrial enterprises organised co-operatively,
2. New service enterprises organised co-operatively,
3. Existing private firms and companies transferring ownership to a co-operative of their workers,
4. Existing state-sponsored bodies and public companies transferring ownership of a subsidiary to co-operatives of its workers,
5. Existing producer co-operatives (agricultural) extending ownership to workers, or transferring ownership of a subsidiary operation to a co-operative of workers,
6. Community development co-operatives of a mixed agricultural/industrial/service nature.

It might also be said, however, that the most fertile ground for the formation of co-operatives is where the existing system is failing to provide an acceptable level of employment and a more satisfying way of life. The most likely place for co-operatives to develop therefore are in urban areas of high unemployment, in under-developed rural areas where already a degree of co-operation exists, as well as among special groups, such as handicapped people.

As a general comment under this heading it should be stated that there are certain sensitive areas in the industrial sector which should be approached warily by co-operative organisers. These are industries suffering from over capacity which IDA are reluctant to grant aid. Examples include: small printing works, clothing and textiles and some areas of the food industry such as new entrants to meat processing, bread baking and fish processing.

Best Corporate Structure for Co-operatives

In his address to the Rome Conference, Paul Derrick (1978) said that in working out its research programme the new British Co-operative Development Agency will have to give priority to a report on the choice of legal forms by those seeking to form new workers' co-operatives. Twenty years ago, he said, this would not have been a problem. It would have been taken for granted that a new co-operative would register under the Industrial and Provident Societies' Acts and the simplest way of doing this would have been to use the Model Rules prepared by Derrick's own organisation, the Co-operative Production Federation (CPF).

Today the situation is rather different, because of the publicity given to the workers' co-operatives at Meriden and KME and the Scott Bader Commonwealth. The latter chose the legal form of a company limited by guarantee rather than by shares. Meriden chose the legal form of a company, limited by shares. A co-operative can also be organised as a partnership in law and some professional partnerships in Britain are set up on a co-operative basis. This form of structure has, however, few advantages for the partners.

It is obvious from the above, therefore, that co-operatives may be formed under a number of different legal structures but it is our opinion that new workers' co-operatives should be established under the Industrial and Provident Societies' Acts, unless there are very good reasons for selecting an alternative structure.

The Industrial and Provident Societies' Acts, both in UK and Ireland, leave considerable discretion regarding the rules to be adopted, but normally it is simpler and cheaper to use the model rules prepared by some promotional body, such as the British Co-operative Production Federation (CPF), the Industrial Common Ownership Movement (ICOM) or the Irish National Co-operative Council (NCC).[18] There is not a great deal to choose, however, between any of these sets of rules. Those designed by the ICOM restrict shareholdings to a £1 share per member. The disadvantage of this rule from the point of view of capital formation has already been mentioned.

The ICOM includes in its rules a clause preventing outsiders holding shares. The rules of the other two bodies do not contain such a clause, but it could easily be included if the organisers of a co-operative so wished. The main disadvantage associated with the rules of CPF and NCC is that they allow the distribution of residual assets to members in proportion to shareholdings. As stated earlier, this can be an incentive to premature dissolution. The rules can, however, be changed easily to prevent this happening.

Derrick (*ibid.*) states that the main thing is to have flexible legislation since the aims of members very considerably depending on the circumstances. Everybody is not of this opinion, however. For instance, Mr John McCarrick, Director General of the ICOS has argued that the Irish legislation is too flexible and because of this some societies registered as co-operatives are not really co-operatives at all. He says that many of the clauses normally included in co-operative rules should be written into the Industrial and Provident Societies' Acts so as to ensure that they are adopted by societies (personal communication, October 1978).

It is not within our competence to offer any detailed suggestions relating to co-operative law, though our researches

[18] The ICOS rules could also be used for workers' co-operatives but they are more appropriate for agricultural societies.

would indicate that a number of broad changes are overdue. We will confine our attentions therefore to outlining some criteria which should guide those framing rules for workers' co-operatives. This will be done by reference to the six basic ICA principles outlined at the beginning of Chapter 2.

1. *Open voluntary membership.* This requires little comment except to say that a person should not be barred from membership because of class or creed and no one should be forced against his or her wishes into joining a co-operative.

2. *Democratic organisation.* This is usually taken to mean one vote for each member, a member being defined as a shareholder. Such an interpretation is incomplete. Democratic organisation has to do with control and the rules should state explicitly:

(i) who should control the society, and
(ii) how that control should be exercised (i.e., method of voting).

With regard to (i) it goes without saying that control should be exercised by members, but in framing rules, societies should be explicit in defining membership. The rules should state:

(a) who should be admitted to membership,
(b) the restrictions which should be placed on members, and
(c) the conditions under which memberships should cease i.e., withdrawal, retirement or expulsion.

Most model rules are very vague on these points. As a result people become members of co-operatives who never should have been admitted in the first place; others remain members long after their usefulness to the society has ceased. As far as *workers' co-operatives* are concerned it is our view that two types of members should be defined.

(a) Full members—workers in the society who have subscribed or are in the process of subscribing a certain number of shares, and
(b) associate members—non-workers who for one reason or

another have subscribed a certain number of shares e.g., local wellwishers or retired workers.

It should be stated in the rules that full members only should have votes and no member should have more than one vote. Associate members should not have votes. In other words, the criterion for control should be usership and people not using the co-operatives have no right to control. The users may, however, if they so wish, co-opt one or two prominent associate members to the Management Committee of the Society if they think that their expertise can be of help in running the co-operative. Such co-opted people should not have votes at general meetings.

3. *Limited Interest on Capital Invested.* The purpose of this rule is to ensure that speculators do not invest money in a successful co-operative and eventually turn it into a capitalistic firm by threats to withdraw investments. Money should be subscribed to co-operatives for the purpose of enabling them to perform the functions they were established for (i.e., for marketing produce, providing jobs, etc.) and not for the purpose of making money on investments. Not everyone agrees, however, with this principle. Many people (including the authors) believe that in order to attract investments the co-operative should be allowed to pay competitive interest rates. After all if it borrows from the bank it must pay bank rates.

4. *Equitable distribution of surpluses.* It is our view that surpluses should be distributed in proportion to members' participation, i.e., as workers or customers but not in proportion to shares held. The biggest difficulty in this connection is in deciding on how much to distribute and how much to plough back. Workers would normally wish to have all surpluses distributed in cash but this would be a dangerous practice. Co-operatives must allocate the bulk of their profits to reserves if they are to survive and careful decisions must therefore be made regarding such allocations.

If a co-operative were to adopt ICOM rules the reserves

would not be classed as "shareholders funds" in the sense that they are in a company and the workers would not benefit from them through increased dividends or higher share prices. In these circumstances the workers may be unwilling to plough profits back. The rules should therefore be framed to allow the workers who earned the surplus (and not other shareholders) to share in it through cash distributions and increased shareholdings.

The Mondragon co-operators argue that personal shareholdings are very important for member involvement but that they are even more important in allowing for participation in the growth of assets. In this connection Derrick says that failure to allow workers purchase shares in the large new co-operatives sponsored by the British government may hinder the success of these organisations. He says that the workers at Meriden Motorcyles are expected to pay back a government loan of £4.2 million over about 15 years, but because they have no personal shareholdings the members will have nothing to show for their heroic efforts when they have done it. It could be argued, of course, that if Meriden had remained under private ownership workers would have nothing to show at any time either but that is another point. Once the business is a co-operative, we believe that members should have some stake in it. It might have been wiser in the long run, therefore, for Meriden to have adopted rules which would allow members to acquire the assets of the firm over time in exchange for the money which they plough back.

Allowing workers to acquire large shareholdings in a co-operative does, however, open up the possibility of their dissolving the firm and sharing out the assets among themselves. There is also the possibility of their turning the business into a limited company. On dissolution, the members should be entitled to take out only as much as they put in with an allowance for inflation. Any accumulated surplus should be given to charity or transferred to another co-operative. It could be argued that rules of this nature would make members reluctant to plough back profits. This, however, depends on the way members view continuing employment in the co-operative. If it can be shown that viability depends on having reasonable reserves, most workers will agree to have such.

The above discussion raises the question of share withdrawal. If a workers' co-operative is to survive workers should not be allowed to withdraw their shares. It is a different matter, however, with retired workers and other non-worker shareholders. In equity they should be entitled to withdraw shares but if a large number of shareholders were to withdraw funds at any one time this action could endanger the viability of the society. It would need to be written into the rules therefore that funds of non-workers are withdrawable but that such drawings should be phased so that the action does not endanger the viability of the society.

5. *Education in co-operative principles.* All commentators on co-operative organisations state that education in co-operative principles is vital if the movement is to develop. Co-operative and potential co-operative workers must be told what the system is about and what they must be prepared to do if they join. When a new co-operative is started in Mondragon all the workers are brought together for two days in isolation and given an intensive course in principles as well as detailed instruction on the operation of their co-operative. At the end of this time anyone who so wishes can leave. Something similar should be done here when a co-operative is founded, but in addition, some kind of continuing education should also be provided.

It is incumbent on the co-operative movement to see that the necessary educational courses are provided. At present the situation in this regard is very unorganised. A number of courses are given at university level both within the colleges and in extra mural centres, but the content of these is very much at the discretion of the lecturers.

Macra na Feirme, Muintir na Tíre and other rural organisations give courses in this topic but here again there is little co-ordination or standardisation of syllabi. The emphasis in all these courses is on rural development and agricultural co-operation. It would appear from the literature that little is taught about workers' co-operatives (O'Brien, 1978). Since October 1978 the Department of Economics in University College, Cork, has been giving a course in "Socialist Labour Managed and Co-operative Economies". It is hoped that this course will stimulate further thinking on co-operatives and their future role.

It is of some interest to note, in this connection, that the ICOS has been pursuing the question of education for many years and has recently established a course for executives from agricultural co-operatives in conjunction with the IMI. In addition it has submitted to the government its views on the need for co-operative education at primary, secondary and tertiary levels and has also had discussions with the different universities and institutes with a view to ensuring that the courses given are relevant. It also intends forming a "Society for Co-operative Studies" with the twin aims of

(a) Promoting an increase in the level and quality of co-operative education and,
(b) co-ordinating research and studies of interest to co-operatives.

If, and when, this Society gets underway it should do much towards improving the standards of co-operative education within the country. This in turn should have the effect of furthering the aims of the co-operative movement generally.*

6. *Co-operation among co-operatives*. This is another vital issue for the success of co-operative development. There are various ways in which one co-operative can help another. They can meet to discuss common problems and ways whereby these problems may be solved. Established co-operatives

* Since this was written a Centre for co-operative studies has been established in University College, Cork.

can give much needed advice to new co-operatives starting up. Financial assistance may also be given by one co-operative to another.

Indeed most writers on the subject of co-operatives agree that co-operatives of all kinds should help each other financially by setting up a bank for co-operatives, where surplus funds could be lodged at commercial rates and which in its turn would examine proposals for the establishment of new co-operatives and fund those found to be potentially viable. It would appear that a co-operative bank is central to any worthwhile co-operative development, particularly that of workers' co-operatives. The establishment of a bank by Irish co-operatives has been suggested on many occasions in recent years but it will be very difficult to get such a bank set up. The conditions attached to obtaining a banking licence are very onerous and the amount of money required to get started is very large. In these circumstances the possibility of having the British or some European co-operative bank established here appears more realistic, and this idea is being investigated.

Additional Services Required for Co-operative Development

The successful launching of workers' co-operatives requires very good organisation. According to Oakeshott (1978, pp. 242-243) the history of co-operative enterprise is as full of lessons about how not to proceed as it is of more positive ones. The majority of democratic enterprises established on working class initiative (Cloth Cap Co-operatives) have remained dwarfish and undynamic despite their surprising survival record. He goes on to say that "the relative lack of success has been due mainly to weak management; they have not been looking for the thrusting young executives—and the thrusting young executives have not been looking for them. To compare their performance with that of capitalist enterprises is thus as Marshall suggested a century ago 'absurd'. We are not comparing like with like".

However, although the record provides valuable guidance

on how to fail, the Spanish experience, in particular, offers more positive lessons. It shows that a number of conditions need to be satisfied if new co-operatives are to have any real chance of long-term success. The following six would appear to be crucial:

1. There must be thorough and systematic preparation and planning in exactly the same way as for capitalistic enterprises
2. the main thrust to get enterprises off the ground must come from the workforce itself and not be imposed from above by politicians or ideologists
3. the commitment of the workforce needs to be further secured by their providing a meaningful capital stake
4. the enterprise must be equipped with a manager or management team which is at least not inferior to that which a conventional enterprise would employ
5. co-operative enterprises must work together in supportive groups, for in isolation they are hopelessly vulnerable. One of the supportive enterprises should ideally be a co-operative bank with a consultancy section attached, and
6. as far as possible, payment to workers should be kept in line with that in comparable employment elsewhere and with similar differentials for different skilled grades.

To ensure that these conditions are at least partially fulfilled some kind of Workers' Co-operative Agency is required. Care must be taken, however, in deciding on the composition of this agency, otherwise it will not perform the functions required. The constitution of the agency and its suggested method of operating are discussed below.

Workers' Co-operative Agency

Co-operation is much more than an activity; it encompasses a philosophy, and this philosophy must be preserved in co-operative activities. In fact, where co-operative principles are not fundamental to an organisation, it becomes an ordinary commercial company. We feel, therefore, that if proper industrial workers' co-operatives are to develop and have a chance of surviving in Ireland they will have to be promoted by a body which is interested in the co-operative ideal. Such a body in addition to organising new societies will also have to develop and co-ordinate educational programmes for the members so as to inculcate in them the necessary degrees of selflessness, caring and pride of accomplishment. Without these attributes the movement has little chance of success.

The promoting body for workers' co-operatives should be called the Workers' Co-operative Agency (WCA) and should be constituted from persons who in the past have been actively associated with the promotion of workers' co-operatives. A few others who have shown themselves to be interested in the co-operative movement generally should also be included as well as a trade unionist and some representatives from relevant state companies such as IDA and AnCO. Care must be exercised, however, in selecting members, because an agency which is not fully committed to workers' co-operatives could easily drift into the organisation of other co-operatives.

Two suggestions have been made to the authors regarding the establishment of the WCA. One is that the initiative should come from the government which would take steps to have the agency established and provided with the necessary funds. The second is that the National Co-operative Council (NCC) should become the development agency and be responsible afterwards for any co-operative formed. At the moment there is a good deal of duplication between the NCC and the ICOS and it has been suggested by a co-ordinating group[19] organised recently by all the national co-operatives that the NCC should concentrate on industrial workers' and similar type organisations and that in fact it should become the suggested Workers' Co-operative Agency.

The authors have no very strong views on this question. There is some merit in both suggestions but regardless of who does the organising the body concerned will need some government aid for the acquisition of premises and the payment of staff. Some formal structures will also need to be established so that financial and other provisions can be co-ordinated with the various state and semi-state employment creating agencies. If the NCC is prepared to set up and work through these structures then it should be given the task of organising the WCA. If, on the other hand, it is unable to work in this way it should leave the organisation to some other group. The agency cannot afford to be haphazard and if it fails the first time it is unlikely to get a second chance.

It is suggested that for a start discussions be held between the government (say, the Department of Industry and Commerce) and the NCC with a view to getting some agreed structure under way and for the purpose of having funds made available by the government on an annual grant-in-aid basis. This grant should be for administrative and consultancy work only. Grants for projects should be channelled through the established agencies in this area (IDA, Gaeltarra Eireann, SFADCO, ICC and IPC, etc.) while for small projects in designated areas there should be access to the Central Development Committee's Special Regional Fund. In the case of the state organisations mentioned above, it would be appropriate for each to designate one staff member as co-operative liaison officer. This official should be trained to deal with the special problems of co-operatives and should be in close contact with the Irish Productivity Centre which has considerable experience of dealing with the problems of worker participation in pri-

[19] This group which consists of representatives of the ICOS, NCC, League of Credit Unions and the National Association of Building Co-operatives has made certain proposals regarding a co-ordinating body for all co-operatives.

vate and semi-state bodies. The liaison officers should in turn form an informal consortium, thereby co-ordinating and streamlining their services to co-operatives. Frequent contact should be maintained with the WCA to ensure that the services provided are as relevant as possible to the needs of co-operatives. In addition to these facilities at national level, the workers' co-operatives should have at local level the County Development Officers to advise and assist them on problems, particularly those of a local dimension.

A further source of advice to the WCA at local or regional level could be provided by setting up advisory groups of interested professionally qualified persons (particularly retired businessmen, accountants, etc.). This could be done on the lines of the Action Resource Centre in the UK and the members could act as advisers or even as temporary managers of newly formed co-operatives. These advisory groups should be organised by the WCA in conjunction with County Development Officers.

A diagrammatic representation of the suggested institutional structure for the Workers' Co-operative Agency is shown in Figure 2.

When the agency has been formed it should set about acquiring premises and staff. The initial appointment should be a whole-time officer to act as secretary. The agency should then set about appointing a development officer. As this officer would need to be familiar with the appraisal of industrial projects it would be preferable for a start to have somebody from the IDA with experience in the small industry's section. The secondment might be for an initial period of two years with an option to renew for a further period, if the operation warrants it.

Duties of the Development Officer

The duties of the development officer should be to contact groups throughout the country who might be interested in forming industrial or service co-operatives. Contact would be

FIGURE 2: Suggested Institutional Structure for Workers' Co-operative Agency

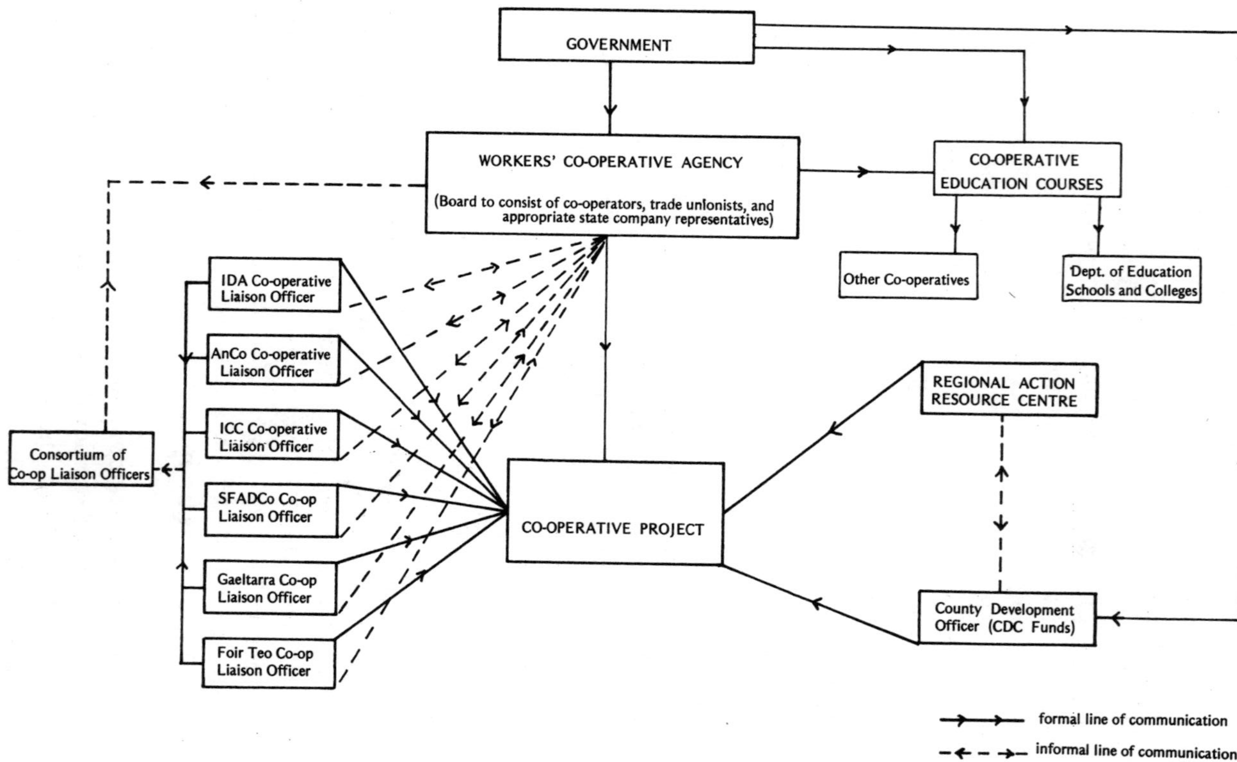

made through agency members and other advisory groups. On visiting a group of interested people the officer should discuss the project with them and ascertain whether or not they had potential for forming a successful co-operative. If it was considered that they had, an objective appraisal of their ideas should be undertaken. In most cases this could be carried out by the development officer himself, but in other cases he might have to call on consultants. Where the appraisal proved favourable projects should be submitted to a relevant agency for funding.

The development officer should also deal with private firms wishing to convert to co-operatives. Firms, which are in financial difficulties, if considered potentially viable should be assessed and treated in the same way as groups starting from scratch. The development agency as a body should keep in touch with all applications by co-operatives for funds to different agencies. If submissions are turned down the agency should examine the reasons so as to ensure that co-operatives are being given the same treatment as other organisations.

We envisage no changes having to be made in IDA services to cope with industrial workers' co-operatives. Submissions from the latter should be treated in exactly the same manner as those from private individuals or companies. We are aware, of course, that the IDA is precluded from funding service industries like building, repairing, transport, etc., on the grounds that any new industries of this kind would be in direct competition with existing services and would probably put some of the latter out of business. Money for co-operative development in the service sector, therefore, will have to come from other state sources such as the Special Regional Fund or from the commercial banks.

Management Assistance

Once formally established, a new workers' co-operative will require the same management expertise as any other enterprise. Advice and assistance in this area should also be organised by the WCA which should see to it that competent people are put in charge. Hence when the establishment of a new co-operative is suggested, the agency should have a large say in the appointment of a manager. If a suitable person is not available provision should be made for having someone located by one of the regional advisory groups, either from among its own members or on secondment from some local firm. This temporary manager should endeavour to locate a permanent manager, either from the co-operative staff or elsewhere, but if he cannot identify such a person, a further temporary manager should be appointed, and so on.

Education

The WCA should liaise with other co-operative organisations, with the Department of Education and the various educational organisations to provide courses in co-operative principles and methods for organisers, members and potential members. It has been suggested that this liaison should be done through the formation of a Society for Co-operative Studies made up of representatives from all co-operative agencies in the state, including the WCA, and the League of Credit Unions.

Remuneration of Managers and Workers

Despite idealistic views to the contrary, it is our view that one of the principal weaknesses of traditional workers' co-operatives has been the narrow wage differentials obtaining. In some cases all workers, skilled and unskilled have received the same basic pay, while in others the differential between the highest and lowest paid has been only 2:1. (In Mondragon the differential allowed is 3:1.) Such pay structures are no doubt suitable for dedicated co-operators. But for the less dedicated, particularly skilled manual and managerial personnel, narrow wage differentials, are not to be recommended. Two things can happen in such cases. The highly skilled people will leave for better paid employment elsewhere at the first available opportunity or else they will seek to have the general wage level in the co-operative raised to uneconomic levels in order to bring their own wage up to those of comparable workers elsewhere in the economy. The latter can very easily happen if the manager feels that his salary is inadequate.

It seems, therefore, that in modern times wage structures in co-operatives should in general be the same as those prevailing in similar private businesses. This applies, in particular, to managerial pay, and if the rules are such that narrow wage differentials must prevail among members, then the manager should not be a member but a hired worker who can be dismissed if he is unable to make the business pay. Indeed, in all co-operatives it is a good idea to have a hired manager; it is much easier to dismiss a paid worker than demote an influential member.

Regardless of who the manager is, the Board of a workers' co-operative must consider very carefully what financial goals should be adopted. The need for a high return on capital to generate funds for investment must be balanced against the desire of the members for high wages, pensions and other benefits. Experience suggests that in a market economy financial strength must be given first priority. At the start at least, therefore, co-operation is no soft option and considerable belt-tightening may be necessary.

Finance

As stated above, the provision of capital is of crucial importance in the development of workers' co-operatives. Traditionally co-operatives have been financed out of members' savings but this method is not adequate in times of inflation. Practically all the co-operatives which have survived in Britain are in industries, such as shoes and clothing manufacture, job printing, and cab operation, which are labour intensive and where the rate of technological change is relatively slow, thus avoiding the need for high capital investment for re-equipment.

In these industries, small units can be relatively efficient. If, however, workers wish to establish more capital intensive units the position is altogether different. In these circumstances the original co-operative principle of capital formation through a common fund built up from members' savings is no longer adequate. Large amounts of capital will be needed at short notice. In theory this capital should come from a co-operative bank but in the immediate future there is little possibility of such a bank being formed. As stated above, funds will therefore have to come from state sources (such as IDA, Gaeltarra Eireann, SFADCO, ICC, Regional Development Fund, etc.). Indeed at the moment this is happening to a large extent in private enterprises. IDA at present grants aid of up to 60 per cent of the capital cost of small industries and if further funds are required the commercial banks generally provide it. In a number of cases small private industries are being set up initially on grants and borrowed capital alone; if the IDA is prepared to grant aid to a small enterprise, the banks will provide the balance of the funding. We understand that the IDA is prepared to offer the same level of funding to industrial workers' co-operatives as it is to private firms and we are informed also that the banks will do likewise if the IDA, some other state agency or a Workers' Co-operative Agency approves of the project. The Trade Union Movement might also be interested in funding one or two co-operatives on an experimental scale.

There should not be too much difficulty, therefore, in funding potentially viable workers' co-operatives. The main difficulty will be in providing a stake for the workers. If the enterprise is to be a real co-operative the workers must have some stake in it, either through investing funds of their own (if they have such) or by putting up borrowed money for which they would be liable. Unfortunately, however, many workers will not have funds nor will they be considered credit worthy by lending institutions. These people will, therefore, have to buy their stake in the business out of wages which may mean a severe imposition for some years. For workers borrowing money the source of funds will usually be the banks or credit unions in areas where the latter are in existence. A credit union can lend finance to a member which can be repaid weekly, over a fixed period. For example, a loan of £1,000 from a credit union can be repaid, along with interest, by payments of £5 per week over five years. In order to foster the co-operative idea the government should make these repayments allowable for tax purposes.

Final Conclusions

Having discussed the development of industrial workers' co-operatives in this and other countries an immediate reaction would be to say that such enterprises have not been outstandingly successful in Western countries generally. Reflection, however, shows that this reaction is not altogether correct. Over the past 150 years, co-operatives have come into existence in many countries in times of depression, when private enterprise failed, and in those periods they have tended to maintain employment in the areas where established and relieved a great deal of human misery. Even in the recent depression, the large British government co-operatives, Meriden and KME, (though the latter has now folded up) have served a useful purpose. They have maintained employment for over 1,000 people who would otherwise have been out of work, and though the cost to the state has been high, this cost is probably less than would have been paid out in unemployment benefits. These businesses have, therefore, done very well in continuing to operate until economic conditions generally have improved.

The fact that a high proportion of workers' co-operatives fail after a period of time should not be taken as an indictment of the movement as a whole. A high proportion of private firms fail also in the early years and co-operatives cannot hope for any greater success. It is our opinion, therefore, that co-operatives have a contribution to make in the creation of employment in Ireland.

Co-operatives should not, of course, be considered as an alternative to private enterprise but rather as a complement to it. If entrepreneurs want to set up their own firms and give employment they should be given every encouragement to do so, but so also should co-operatives. The latter may well be the coming form of business organisation in a world which has difficulty in providing full employment and which cannot control industrial disputes.

REFERENCES

ADIZES, Ichak and Elizabeth MANN BORGESE, 1975. *Self Management: New Dimensions to Democracy*, Center for the Study of Democratic Institutions. Santa Barbara, California and Oxford.

BARKAI, Haim, 1977. *Growth Patterns of the Kibbutz Economy*, New York: North Holland.

BARKAI, Haim, 1978. "Incentives, Efficiency and Social Control: The Case of the Kibbutz", *The Maurice Falk Institute for Economic Research in Israel.* Discussion paper 7815, Jerusalem, October.

BAYARD, T., D. ELAM, C. FANNING, S. KELMAN, D. MUELLER, R. SCHRAMM, J. VANEK, and W.F. WHYTE, 1974. "Toward a Fully Self-Managed Industrial Sector in the United States", New York: *Administration and Society*, Vol. 7, No. 1, May.

BELLAS, Carl, J., 1972. *Industrial Democracy and the Worker-Owned Firm*, New York: Praeger.

BLUMBERG, Paul, 1968. *Industrial Democracy: The Sociology of Participation*, New York: Schochen.

BOGGIS, Fred, 1973. "Workers' Co-operatives: A Vital Experiment", in *Participation in Industry*, Campbell Balfour (ed.), London: Croon Helm.

BOLGER, Patrick, 1977. *The Irish Co-operative Movement, its History and Development*, Dublin: Institute of Public Administration.

BRUCE-GARDYNE, Jock, 1978. *Meriden: Odyssey of a Lame Duck*, London: Centre for Policy Studies.

CAMPBELL, Alastair and Blair FOSTER, 1974. "The Mondragon Movement: Worker Ownership in Modern Industry", London: *Industrial Common Ownership Movement (ICOM)*, Pamphlet No. 5, November.

CAMPBELL, Alastair, 1976. "Worker Ownership", *Industrial Common Ownership Movement*, London.

CAMPBELL, Alastair, Charles KEEN, Geraldine NORMAN and Robert OAKESHOTT, 1977. *Worker-Owners: The Mondragon Achievement*, London: Anglo-German Foundation for the Study of Industrial Society.

CHAPLIN, Paul and Roger COWE, 1977. "A Survey of Contemporary British Worker Co-operatives", *Manchester Business School and Centre for Business Research*, Working Paper Series, 36.

CURRAN, James and John STANWORTH, 1979. "Worker Involvement and Social Relations in the Small Firm", Keele: *Sociological Review*, Vol. 27, No. 2, May.

DANIEL, Abraham, 1976. *Labour Enterprises in Israel*, Volume I.

International Center of Research and Information on Public and Co-operative Economy. Jerusalem: Academic Press.

DERRICK, Paul, 1978. "Prospects for Industrial Co-operatives", *Co-op Review*, July.

DERRICK, Paul, 1979. "The Times: A Comparative Solution", *Review of International Co-operation*, Vol. 72, No. 2, London: International Co-operative Alliance.

EYNON, David, 1978. "The Position of the Co-operative Movement in Northern Ireland Today", Paper read to Conference on Co-operatives in Northern Ireland, Magee College, Londonderry, 10 November.

FRAMEWORK FOR CO-OPERATIVE DEVELOPMENT, 1979. Paper put before the Co-operative Movement in Ireland by the *Council of the Irish Agricultural Organisation Society*, Dublin: Burlington Hotel, January.

HMSO, 1977, *Report of the Working Group on a Co-operative Development Agency*, London: Cmnd. 6972, October.

IRISH AGRICULTURAL ORGANISATION SOCIETY, *Annual Reports for various years*, Dublin: Plunkett House, 84 Merrion Square.

JAY, Peter, 1976. "Employment, Inflation and Politics", Sixth Wincott Lecture, London: *Institute of Economic Affairs.*

JENKINS, David, 1973. *Job Power, Blue and White Collar Democracy*, New York: Doubleday.

JOHNSON, A.G., and W.F. WHYTE, 1977. "The Mondragon System of Worker Production Co-operatives", Ithaca (Cornell University): *Industrial and Labour Relations Review*, Vol. 31, No. 1, October.

JONES, Derek, C., 1974. *The Economics of British Producer Co-operatives*, Unpublished Ph.D. Thesis, Cornell University, USA.

JONES, Derek, C., 1978. "Producer Co-operatives in Industrialised Western Economies: An Overview", Belgium: *Annals of Public and Co-operative Economy*, Vol. 49, No. 2, April-June.

KAMUSIC, M., 1970. "Economic Efficiency and Workers' Self-Management", in Yugoslavia: *Workers' Self-Management*, by M.J. Brockmeyer, (ed.) Holland: Reidel, Dordrecht.

KAVCIC, B., 1974. "The System of Self-Management in Yugoslavian Work Organisation", Lecture at Summer Course on Industrial Democracy in University College, Cork, 15-19 July.

KENNEDY, K.A., 1976. "Impressions of Israel", Dublin: *The Economic and Social Research Institute*, Reprint Series, No. 47.

KENT, Bruce, 1977. *Co-operation in Glencolumbkille: A Social and Economic Study*, Honours degree thesis, Coleraine: New University of Ulster, March.

KESTER, Gerard, 1979. "Transition to Workers' Self-Management: Its

dynamics in the decolonizing economy of Malta", The Hague: *Institute of Social Studies*, Report No. 7.
KLATZMANN, Joseph, 1963. *Les Enseignements de L'Experience Israelienne*, Paris: Presses Universitaries de France, p.9.
LOSH, L., 1979. "Fifty Years of the Co-operative Centre—Producers and Services Co-operatives in Israel", London: *Review of International Co-operation* Vol. 72, No. 2.
McKAY, R. and B. BARR, 1976. *The Story of the Scottish Daily News*, Edinburgh: Cannongate.
MEADE, James, 1972. "The Theory of Labour Managed Firms and of Profit Sharing", London: *The Economic Journal*, Vol. 82, No. 325S, March (Supplement).
MELMAN, S., 1969. "Industrial Efficiency under Managerial versus Co-operative Decision-Making", in Horvat, B., *et al. Self Governing Socialism*, New York: International Arts and Sciences Press, Vol. 2.
MILLAR, R.F., 1978. "Worker Self-Management in Yugoslavia: The Current State of Play", Australia: *Journal of Industrial Relations*, September.
MORTENSEN, Peter, 1977. *Labour Co-operatives in Denmark in The Danish Co-operative Movement*, Copenhagen: The Danish Institute.
MURPHY, C., 1970. "Management and Industrial Relations in Ireland", Address at opening of Industrial Sociology Congress at University College Galway, January 14.
NEWBY, Howard, 1977. "Paternalism and Capitalism", in Richard Scase (ed.) *Industrial Society, Class, Cleavage and Control*, London: Allen and Unwin.
"No More Nationalisation", 1978. *The Economist*, 3 June.
OAKESHOTT, Robert, 1978. *The Case for Workers' Co-operatives*, London: Routledge and Kegan Paul.
O'BRIEN, T., 1978. "Co-operation in Ireland", Source Document No. 1, Coleraine: *The New University of Ulster*, Institute of Continuing Education.
O'MAHONY, David, 1973. "The Participatory Economy", Dublin: *Studies*, Spring issue.
——————, 1979. "Labour Management and the Market Economy", Dublin: *Irish Journal of Business and Administrative Research*, Vol. 1, No. 1, April.
PEARSE, John, 1977. "An Industrial Experiment in Cumbria", Papers in Community Studies No. 13, *University of York*, Department of Social Administration and Social Work.
PEDERSON, Clements, 1977. *The Danish Co-operative Movement*, Copenhagen: The Danish Institute.

PRAIS, S.J., 1978. "The Strike Proneness of Large Plants in Britain", London: *Journal of the Royal Statistical Society*, Series A. Vol. 141, Part 3.

Report of the International Co-operative Alliance Congress, 1966.

SPENCER, Ray, 1978. "Co-op Bank gives a Boost to Workers' Co-operatives", Manchester: Press notice, *Cooperative Bank Ltd.*, New Century House, 11 July.

SHOREY, J., 1975. "The Size of Work Unit and Strike Incidence", Oxford: *Journal of Industrial Economics*, Vol. 23, No. 3.

SMITH, Arthur, 1978. "Meriden faces a long hard ride", *The Financial Times*, Friday, 20 January.

STATIONERY OFFICE, *Economic and Social Development 1976-1980*, 1976, Dublin, September, Prl. 5.758.

STEINHERR, Alfred and Jaroslav VANEK, 1974. "Self Management as a European Strategy", *Working Paper No. 7407*, Department Trevail, Institute des Sciences Economics, Louvain, Belgium.

STETTNER, Leonora, 1977. "The Role of Co-operatives in Israel", London: *Review of International Co-operation*, Vol. 70, No. 2.

——————, 1979. "Trade Unions and Co-operatives in Partnership—The Danish Experience", London: *Review of International Co-operation* Vol. 72, No. 2.

SWEETMAN, R., 1972. *On Our Knees*, London: Pan.

The Co-operative Movement in Denmark, 1970. Copenhagen: The Central Co-operative Committee of Denmark, The Central Union of Urban Co-operative Societies, and The Danish Co-operative Wholesale Society.

TURNER, H.A., 1969. *Is Britain Really Strike Prone?* Cambridge: University Press.

VANEK, Jaroslav, 1969. "Decentralisation under Workers' Management: A Theoretical Appraisal", New York: *American Eceonomic Review*, Vol. 59, No. 5.

——————, 1970. *The General Theory of Labour Managed Market Economies*, Ithaca (New York): Cornell University Press.

——————, 1971. *The Participatory Economy*, Ithaca (New York): Cornell University Press.

WEBB, Beatrice and Sydney, 1921. *Constitution for the Socialist Commonwealth of Great Britain*, London: Longmans.

APPENDIX

List of people who supplied oral and written information relating to co-operatives

G. Cashman, Graphic Arts Co-operative, Dublin.
O. Travers, Crannac Co-operative, Navan.
W. Elliot, Irish Springs Co-operative, Dundalk.
R. Wait, Castle Shoes Co-operative, Dundalk.
V. Bewley, Bewley's Cafes, Dublin.
P. Ó nAolain, and T. de Blachain, Comharchumann Chois Fharraige, Galway.
P. Wallis, Clover Meats Co-operative, Waterford.
Very Rev. J. McDyer, P.P., Glencolumbkille Co-operative, Donegal.
Very Rev. G. Campbell, P.P., Ballymackney, Dundalk.
N. Herlihy and M. O'Doherty, Irish League of Credit Unions, Dublin.
B. Thomson, National Association of Building Co-operatives, Dublin.
P. Bolger and J. Moloney, ICOS, Dublin.
J. O'Halloran and B. Ó Cearbhaill, National Co-operative Council, Dublin.
J. O'Mahoney and P. McCarrick, North Connacht Farmers' Co-operative, Tubercurry, Co. Sligo.
P. Donnelly, IDA, Dublin.
D. Wills, IMI, Dublin.
M. Aherne, Department of Labour, Dublin.
M. Dorgan and A. Coldrick, AnCO, Dublin.
Professor D.I.F. Lucey and Dr. C. Fanning, University College, Cork.

C. Murphy, Rights Commissioner, Dublin.

D. Eynon, Local Enterprise Development Unit, Belfast.

K. McManus and B. Smearton, Cope News, Belfast.

T. O'Brien and Dr L. Kennedy, New University of Ulster, Coleraine, Co. Londonderry.

W.E. Caughey, Department of Commerce, Belfast.

Professor D. Rea, Ulster Polytechnic, Belfast.

F. Dologhan, Newry and Mourne Co-operative Society, Newry.

J. Loughran, Department of Manpower Services, Belfast.

F. Cahill, Whiterock Pictures, Belfast.

T. McIlwaine, Northern Counties Co-operative, Swatragh, Co. Down.

Rev. N. O'Grady, Edenard Enterprises, Belfast.

I. Brierley, Cooperative Bank Ltd., Manchester.

P. Derrick, International Co-operative Alliance, London.

B. Shedden, Central Council for Agricultural and Horticultural Co-operation, London.

J.A. Walter, Executive Registrar, Registry of Friendly Societies, London.

P. Chaplin, Manchester Business School, Manchester.

C. Campbell, Scottish Workers' Co-operative Council, Glasgow.

Dr T. Barzilai, Director, Institute for Social and Economic Research, General Federation of Labour, Tel Aviv, Israel.

Members of the Empressarial Division of the Mondragon Co-operative who kindly explained the movement to the Irish delegation who visited Mondragon in October 1978.

J. Hogarty, Commercial Attaché, Royal Danish Embassy, Dublin.

Danish Central Co-operative Committee, Copenhagen.

Danish Central Union of Urban Co-operatives, Copenhagen.

Italian Embassy, Dublin.

P. Slowe, Co-operative Development Agency, London.

R. Oakeshott, Job Ownership Ltd., London.

Annual Report, Northern Ireland Counties' Co-operatives.

THE ECONOMIC AND SOCIAL RESEARCH INSTITUTE

Books:

Economic Growth in Ireland: The Experience Since 1947
Kieran A. Kennedy and Brendan Dowling

Irish Economic Policy: A Review of Major Issues
Staff Members of ESRI (eds. B. R. Dowling and J. Durkan)

Policy Research Series:

1. *Regional Policy and the Full-Employment Target* — M. Ross and B. Walsh
2. *Energy Demand in Ireland, Projections and Policy Issues* — S. Scott

Broadsheet Series:

1. *Dental Services in Ireland* — P. R. Kaim-Caudle
2. *We Can Stop Rising Prices* — M. P. Fogarty
3. *Pharmaceutical Services in Ireland* — P. R. Kaim-Caudle
assisted by Annette O'Toole and Kathleen O'Donoghue
4. *Ophthalmic Services in Ireland* — P. R. Kaim-Caudle
assisted by Kathleen O'Donoghue and Annette O'Toole
5. *Irish Pensions Schemes,* 1969 — P. R. Kaim-Caudle and J. G. Byrne
assisted by Annette O'Toole
6. *The Social Science Percentage Nuisance* — R. C. Geary
7. *Poverty in Ireland: Research Priorities* — Brendan M. Walsh
8. *Irish Entrepreneurs Speak for Themselves* — M. P. Fogarty
9. *Marital Desertion in Dublin: an exploratory study* — Kathleen O'Higgins
10. *Equalization of Opportunity in Ireland: Statistical Aspects*
R. C. Geary and F. S. Ó Muircheartaigh
11. *Public Social Expenditure in Ireland* — Finola Kennedy
12. *Problems in Economic Planning and Policy Formation in Ireland,* 1958–1974
Desmond Norton
13. *Crisis in the Cattle Industry* — R. O'Connor and P. Keogh
14. *A Study of Schemes for the Relief of Unemployment in Ireland*
R. C. Geary and M. Dempsey
with Appendix — E. Costa
15. *Dublin Simon Community,* 1971–1976: *an Exploration* — Ian Hart
16. *Aspects of the Swedish Economy and their relevance to Ireland*
Robert O'Connor, Eoin O'Malley and Anthony Foley
17. *The Irish Housing System: A Critical Overview* — T. J. Baker and L. M. O'Brien
18. *The Irish Itinerants: Some Demographic, Economic and Educational Aspects*
M. Dempsey and R. C. Geary
19. *A Study of Industrial Workers' Co-operatives* — Robert O'Connor and Philip Kelly

General Research Series

1. *The ownership of Personal Property in Ireland* — Edward Nevin
2. *Short-Term Economic Forecasting and its Application in Ireland* — Alfred Kuehn
3. *The Irish Tariff and The E.E.C.: A Factual Survey* — Edward Nevin
4. *Demand Relationships for Ireland* — C. E. V. Leser
5. *Local Government Finance in Ireland: A Preliminary Survey* — David Walker
6. *Prospects of the Irish Economy in* 1962 — Alfred Kuehn
7. *The Irish Woollen and Worsted Industry,* 1946–59: *A Study in Statistical Method*
R. C. Geary
8. *The Allocation of Public Funds for Social Development* — David Walker
9. *The Irish Price Level: A Comparative Study* — Edward Nevin
10. *Inland Transport in Ireland: A Factual Survey* — D. J. Reynolds
11. *Public Debt and Economic Development* — Edward Nevin
12. *Wages in Ireland,* 1946–62 — Edward Nevin
13. *Road Transport: The Problems and Prospects in Ireland* — D. J. Reynolds

14. *Imports and Economic Growth in Ireland,* 1947–61 — C. E. V. Leser
15. *The Irish Economy in* 1962 *and* 1963 — C. E. V. Leser
16. *Irish County Incomes in* 1960 — E. A. Attwood and R. C. Geary
17. *The Capital Stock of Irish Industry* — Edward Nevin
18. *Local Government Finance and County Incomes* — David Walker
19. *Industrial Relations in Ireland: The Background* — David O'Mahony
20. *Social Security in Ireland and Western Europe* — P. R. Kaim-Caudle
21. *The Irish Economy in* 1963 *and* 1964 — C. E. V. Leser
22. *The Cost Structure of Irish Industry* 1950–60 — Edward Nevin
23. *A Further Analysis of Irish Household Budget Data,* 1951–1952 — C. E. V. Leser
24. *Economic Aspects of Industrial Relations* — David O'Mahony
25. *Psychological Barriers to Economic Achievement* — P. Pentony
26. *Seasonality in Irish Economic Statistics* — C. E. V. Leser
27. *The Irish Economy in* 1964 *and* 1965 — C. E. V. Leser
28. *Housing in Ireland: Some Economic Aspects* — P. R. Kaim-Caudle
29. *A Statistical Study of Wages, Prices and Employment in the Irish Manufacturing Sector* — C. St. J. O'Herlihy
30. *Fuel and Power in Ireland: Part I. Energy Consumption in* 1970 — J. L. Booth
31. *Determinants of Wage Inflation in Ireland* — Keith Cowling
32. *Regional Employment Patterns in the Republic of Ireland* — T.J. Baker
33. *The Irish Economy in* 1966 — The Staff of The Economic Research Institute
34. *Fuel and Power in Ireland: Part II. Electricity and Turf* — J.L. Booth
35. *Fuel and Power in Ireland: Part III. International and Temporal Aspects of Energy Consumption* — J. L. Booth
36. *Institutional Aspects of Commercial and Central Banking in Ireland* — John Hein
37. *Fuel and Power in Ireland: Part IV. Sources and Uses of Energy* — J. L. Booth
38. *A Study of Imports* — C. E. V. Leser
39. *The Irish Economy in* 1967 — The Staff of The Economic and Social Research Institute
40. *Some Aspects of Price Inflation in Ireland* — R. C. Geary and J. L. Pratschke
41. *A Medium Term Planning Model for Ireland* — David Simpson
42. *Some Irish Population Problems Reconsidered* — Brendan M. Walsh
43. *The Irish Brain Drain* — Richard Lynn
44. *A Method of Estimating the Stock of Capital in Northern Ireland Manufacturing Industry: Limitations and Applications* — C. W. Jefferson
45. *An Input-Output Analysis of the Agricultural Sector of the Irish Economy in* 1964 — R. O'Connor with M. Breslin
46. *The Implications for Cattle Producers of Seasonal Price Fluctuations* — R. O'Connor
47. *Transport in the Developing Economy of Ireland* — John Blackwell
48. *Social Status and Inter-Generational Social Mobility in Dublin* — Bertram Hutchinson
49. *Personal Incomes by County,* 1965 — Miceal Ross
50. *Income-Expenditure Relations in Ireland,* 1965–1966 — John L. Pratschke
51. *Costs and Prices in Transportable Goods Industries* — W. Black, J. V. Simpson, D. G. Slattery
52. *Certain Aspects of Non-Agricultural Unemployment in Ireland* — R. C. Geary and J. G. Hughes
53. *A Study of Demand Elasticities for Irish Imports* — Dermot McAleese
54. *Internal Migration in Ireland* — R. C. Geary and J. G. Hughes
    with Appendix — C. J. Gillman
55. *Religion and Demographic Behaviour in Ireland* — B. M. Walsh
    with Appendix — R. C. Geary and J. G. Hughes
56. *Views on Pay Increases, Fringe Benefits and Low Pay* — H. Behrend, A. Knowles and J. Davies
57. *Views on Income Differentials and the Economic Situation* — H. Behrend, A. Knowles and J. Davies
58. *Computers in Ireland* — F. G. Foster
59. *National Differences in Anxiety* — Richard Lynn

60. *Capital Statistics for Irish Manufacturing Industry* C. W. Jefferson
61. *Rural Household Budget—Feasability Study* Sile Sheehy and R. O'Connor
62. *Effective Tariffs and the Structure of Industrial Protection in Ireland* Dermot McAleese
63. *Methodology of Personal Income Estimation by County* Miceal Ross
64. *Further Data on County Incomes in the Sixties* Miceal Ross
65. *The Functional Distribution of Income in Ireland,* 1938–70 J. G. Hughes
66. *Irish Input-Output Structures,* 1964 *and* 1968 E. W. Henry
67. *Social Status in Dublin: Marriage, Mobility and First Employeemnt* Bertram Hutchison
68. *An Economic Evaluation of Irish Salmon Fishing, I: The Visiting Anglers* R. O'Connor and B. J. Whelan
69. *Women and Employment in Ireland: Results of a National Survey* Brendan M. Walsh assisted by Annette O'Toole
70. *Irish Manufactured Imports from the UK in the Sixties: The Effects of AIFTA* Dermot McAleese and John Martin
71. *Alphabetical Voting: A Study of the* 1973 *General Election in the Republic of Ireland* Christopher Robson and Brendan M. Walsh
72. *A Study of the Irish Cattle and Beef Industries* Terence J. Baker, Robert O'Connor and Rory Dunne
73. *Regional Employment Patterns in Northern Ireland* William Black and Clifford W. Jefferson
74. *Irish Full Employment Structures,* 1968 *and* 1975 E. W. Henry
75. *An Economic Evaluation of Irish Salmon Fishing II: The Irish Anglers* R. O'Connor, B. J. Whelan and A. McCashin
76. *Factors Relating to Reconviction among Young Dublin Probationers* Ian Hart
77. *The Structure of Unemployment in Ireland,* 1954–1972 Brendan M. Walsh
78. *An Economic Evaluation of Irish Salmon Fishing, III: The Commercial Fishermen* B. J. Whelan, R. O'Connor, and A. McCashin
79. *Wage Inflation and Wage Leadership* W. E. J. McCarthy, J. F. O'Brien and V. G. Dowd
80. *An Econometric Study of the Irish Postal Services* Peter Neary
81. *Employment Relationships in Irish Counties* Terence J. Baker and Miceal Ross
82. *Irish Input-Output Income Multipliers* 1964 *and* 1968 J. R. Copeland and E. W. Henry
83. *A Study of the Structural and Determinants of the Behavioural Component of Social Attitudes in Ireland* E. E. Davis
84. *Economic Aspects of Local Authority Expenditure and Finance* J. R. Copeland and Brendan M. Walsh
85. *Population Growth and other Statistics of Middle-sized Irish Towns* D. Curtin, R. C. Geary, T. A. Grimes and B. Menton
86. *The Income Sensitivity of the Personal Income Tax Base in Ireland,* 1947–1972 Brendan R. Dowling
87. *Traditional Families? From Culturally Prescribed to Negotiated Roles in Farm Families* Damian F. Hannan and Louise Katsiaouni
88. *An Irish Personality Differential: A Technique for Measuring Affective and Cognitive Dimensions of Attitudes Towards Persons* E. E. Davis and Mary O'Neill
89. *Redundancy and Re-Employment in Ireland* Brendan J. Whelan and Brendan M. Walsh
90. *A National Model of Fuel Allocation—A Prototype* E. W. Henry and S. Scott
91. *A Linear Programming Model for Irish Agriculture* Robert O'Connor, Miceal Ross and Michael Behan
92. *Irish Educational Expeditures—Past Present and Future* A. Dale Tussing
93. *The Working and Living Conditions of Civil Service Typists* Nóirin O Broin and Gillian Farren
94. *Irish Public Debt* Richard Bruton
95. *Output and Employment in the Irish Food Industry to* 1990 A. D. O'Rourke and T. M. McStay
96. *Displacement and Development: Class, Kinship and Social Change in Irish Rural*

Communities Damian F. Hannan

97. *Attitudes in the Republic of Ireland relevant to the Northern Ireland problem: Vol. 1: Descriptive analysis and some comparisons with Attitudes in Northern Ireland and Great Britian* E. E. Davis and R. Sinnott

98. *Internal Migration Flows in Ireland and their Determinants* J. G. Hughes and B. M. Walsh

99. *Irish Input-Output Structures,* 1976 E. W. Henry